DREAMS

HOW TO INTERPRET GOD'S MESSAGES

EJ HILLMAN

Hillman Publishing

HP

Front cover design by Emily-Jane Hillman and Simon Hillman from an original painting by Emily-Jane Hillman

Published by:
Hillman Publishing
Email: ej@ejhillman.com
Web: www.ejhillman.com

ISBN 978-1-909996-17-5

Testimonials

Emily-Jane Hillman's insights in "Dreams — How to Interpret God's Messages" are nothing short of divine revelation. With a spirit-led heart and an unwavering dedication to waiting on the Holy Spirit, Emily navigates the intricate world of dreams with unparalleled accuracy. Her interpretations offer a profound glimpse into the mysteries of the Kingdom, making this book a must-read for anyone seeking deeper spiritual understanding.
—Melanie, Chicago

As the world rediscovers the value of dreams and the importance of dream interpretation, this book comes at the perfect time. Without error, Emily-Jane Hillman is one of the most gifted dream interpreters of our time. Her ability to hear a dream, interpret it, and release an activation for the dreamer is unparalleled. The wisdom and understanding she has collected over the years make this book a staple in the collection of all serious dream interpreters.
—Aracely, Texas

Emily-Jane has a unique and special anointing for dream interpretation. I've been blessed by her ability to hear the Lord and interpret dreams for myself and others. I've seen the Lord speak through her to unlock mysteries that have challenged and provoked a deeper understanding and excitement for God's heart as His plans for the future unfold through our dreams.
—Tausha, Seattle

Emily-Jane is an incredible gifted dream interpreter and her wealth of biblical knowledge and depth of wisdom always leaves me amazed on the simple revelation that comes when I've given her a dream. I can't wait to read her book and help me decipher my own dreams using her expertise and years of practice.
—Olivia, UK

Emily-Jane has been a great help to me regarding dreams. I had been asking God to give me dreams in the night for a long time, and when Emily-Jane prayed for me, I had a dream a few nights later. It seemed a very straightforward one in terms of meaning and message, but when I shared it with her, she explained the meaning of the symbols and thus unpacked a much more detailed message than what it was at first glance.
—Krisztina, Hungary

Other Books by the Author (Emily Barroso)

Big Men's Boots – The Way

Unless a Seed Falls to the Ground

Acknowledgements

Thank you to all those that encouraged me to write this book. You know who you are. Thank you to all of you who have trusted me to interpret your dreams. I could not have written this book without the wisdom and counsel of my husband, Dr Simon Richard Hillman who gently corrects me, sharpens me with his wisdom and counsel and challenges me to be the best person I can be. And with whom, along with our children, we interpret dreams daily.

For Grace Elizabeth, our daughter of promise

Introduction..9

A Note for people who might not believe in God..................15

Chapter 1. The Vital Importance of Dreams to the Body of Christ..23

Chapter 2. How God Speaks through Dreams.........................29

Chapter 3. What are Dreams and Visions Exactly?...............40

Chapter 4. Bible Dreamers..52

Chapter 5. Who is Qualified to Interpret Dreams? 59

Chapter 6. Dream Sources..68

Chapter 7. Discerning Good from Evil: The Counterfeit.....78

Chapter 8. Dream Types..89

Chapter 9. All the Wonderful Things That God Can Do! ..100

Chapter 10. We are Required to Interpret Dreams and not Translate them 120

Chapter 11. Biblical Parables 129

Chapter 12. Skillset..135

Chapter 13. Dreams are Personal.....................................143

Chapter 14. Prepare to Dream...156

Chapter 15. Decoding 165

Chapter 16. Mining for Revelation: National and International Dreams 174

Chapter 17. Interpretation Toolkit 193

Final Questions & Other Considerations............................206

Symbology Key for the meaning of the parable:................210

Introduction

"The Word became flesh and made his dwelling among us. We have seen his glory, the glory of the one and only Son, who came from the Father, full of grace and truth."
John 1:14

When was the last time you remembered, or better, recorded one of your dreams? Over and over again, the Bible shows us that God communicates directly with us through dreams and visions, yet relatively few believers are interested in this mysterious way that God delivers life changing information. He speaks an eternal language after all. God has always hungered for relationship with humanity, the pinnacle of His creation. The Bible shows us that God has been communicating with people since the dawn of time and He will continue to do so until the eve of time and beyond time. He spoke first through his creation, then 'face to face' with Adam and Eve before the fall, and then via the prophets, priests and poets of the Old Testament. Later He spoke through the apostles and teachers of the New Testament, and, since His ascension, Jesus communicates with us through the Holy Spirit who resides in the spirits (the hearts) of believers, often as "the still small voice," described by the prophet Elijah. All humanity have the facility but not necessarily the ability to hear from God. Today, God still communicates through prophets and apostles, and via the song, poetry and exposition of the Bible. His word is eternal. He has also consistently, and to this day, sent angels as messengers, or ministering spirits to help us. In order to hear the way God speaks we need to be 'tuned in' to the method of visual language that God uses. The Bible calls this having 'ears to hear and eyes to see':

9

"But blessed are your eyes because they see, and your ears because they hear," (Matthew 13:16). So many of us ignore these messages from the eternal kingdom, and as such potentially miss out on extraordinary growth opportunities, direction, breakthroughs and life changing advice. From Abraham's call to the promised land, to its confirmation in a dream to His son Jacob, that led to God's covenant with and the formation of the state of Israel as we know it today, to the birth, death and resurrection of the Messiah that was directed by five dreams and three visions, God has been directing and revealing world changing knowledge to humankind through dreams and visions. How much stronger and better might individual believers and the church at large, the *ekklesia,* be if only they paid heed to this profound way that God speaks? There is much documented evidence of people receiving creative breakthroughs through dreams in our day and of God speaking to non believers in the Bible. As such, this book is not only for 'dreamers' it is for every believer. Not just for prophets and seers, but for all who have 'ears to hear and eyes to see,' which is you. This book has been written to equip you with wisdom for the days ahead. For these are the last days foretold by the prophet, Joel: "In the last days, God says, I will pour out my Spirit on all people. Your sons and daughters will prophesy, your young men will see visions, your old men will dream dreams." This is you. But I don't dream! I hear you say. You do. Everyone does - this is what happens in the REM stage of sleep, when your eyes are moving from left to right, watching God's movie on the screen of your mind. You simply need help REMembering them! But we dream throughout the night too. I'll help with that later. Now is the time to learn God's dream language. These are the last days! Wake up to dreaming! Expand your knowledge and understanding of dreams and God will cause you to dream bigger! "For whoever has will be given more, and they will have an abundance. Whoever does not have, even what they have will be taken from them." (Matthew 29:25). Don't miss out on the eternal shout out!

Before we dive into the eternal language of dreams, visions and parables, I will tell you a little about myself and the code I try to live by before explaining how to decode dreams and visions, so that you can judge whether you're in safe hands. I have had dreams since I was a tiny child and have been interpreting my own dreams for almost a quarter of a century. I became a believer at the close of 2000/ early 2001, after an adventurous adult life that included being a fashion model and a singer in a Camden indie-rock band before my life was turned around, after which I became an award winning author and artist, teacher and coach. When I committed to being a follower of Jesus, I was 32 and had a toddler who is now 27 and marvellous, as are my other three younger children. All gifts from God, so I take no credit apart from stewarding my responsibility as well as possible. (I don't hilariously boast that I 'created them' like some Hollywood celebrities that I can think of.) I was a single mother living in Camden Town in London, which is a groovy part of town. I was busy getting a teaching qualification, in between my first degree, a BA (Hons) in English Literature and my second Masters Degree in Creative Writing. I was shortly to receive a national book award for my first book, *After the Rains*, a novel, set in the Rhodesia/Zimbabwe civil war, by which vehicle I embarked on a career in writing, literary editing (developing books for clients) publishing and teaching creative writing and the arts in a therapeutic context. I have made a film on artists in exile in Burma for English PEN and have directed arts festivals and charities and written, produced and directed plays in London and Wales. Suffice to say, I am a creative child of God (the master creator) who does not like to stay in any lane, and certainly not a prescribed one. I understand the language of metaphor and symbols very well given my arts training, and my study of Literature and Creative Writing along with Psychoanalysis, Poetry and playwriting at university and in professional capacity, training that has lent itself well to being a dream interpreter given the language of dreams and visions is symbolic and intuitive - or '*intune*ative'—(I made that word up!) in tune with the Holy Spirit. I have a special interest in the power of creativity in holistic healing and have operated as a seer prophet (see the Bible for more on seer prophets) and dream interpreter for decades. In Greek, the original language of the New Testament, two different Greek words are used to refer to the word of God: *logos,* from which we get 'log' as in record and the other is *rhema.* Both *logos* and *rhema* are the Word of God, but the former is God's Word spoken objectively, or to mankind as recorded in the Bible, while the latter is the word of God spoken to us, personally, at a specific occasion, or arriving just at the right time, which feels subjective and immediate. I love the written record of the word of God in the Bible and the active, living word of God as revealed by Jesus - both the *logos* and *rhema.* We utilise both aspects of God in dream interpretation. When I became a believer during my studies, it was as a result of a vision and a set of 'Godly incidences' sometimes dismissed as coincidences. Thereafter He continued to speak to me and direct me in dreams and visions. No wonder my life improved drastically! So much so for the better that I began achieving things I would not have had the confidence, to pull off alone (without God, basically) much start a kids party businesses with a number of celebrity clients. I also became in-house chef at Tomboy Films all the while raising my son alone with no financial or other support from his father or any family members while I studied at the same time. This sounds like a boast but I boast in God as I could never have pulled off getting several degrees, a teaching qualification and a national book award, acquiring a literary agent and publishing a book, whilst running independent businesses and raising a child single handedly. But I did nothing single handedly. God, through the power of the Holy Spirit gave me the power to achieve things I could not have achieved in my own strength. He began to heal me from a traumatic childhood and its outworking: abuse, neglect and cancer. He coloured my world with joy and infinite possibility and cured me from acute depression and got me through other momentous events that could have been catastrophic. The Bible makes clear that becoming a believer does not necessarily mean a life of picnics and skipping through the fields with a crown of daisies on one's head, though this does and has happened. I have walked through very tough times as a believer but have done so in victory and have come out stronger as opposed to crushed as I was before I knew God.

I hope you will find what I have to say useful if you are curious. I've tried to write in plain language for a variety of cultures and backgrounds and to limit the 'Christianese' so that it is accessible to all, regardless of denomination or church background, or indeed no church background. I use the word 'God' to refer to the tripartite God rather than His many names, to make things straightforward, and the Holy Spirit for the revelation we get subjectively, through dreams and visions. In writing this book, I hope to convey, as practically and unfussily as possible that all you need to interpret dreams is a willing and humble spirit, a Bible, notebook and pen, and the revelation of the Holy Spirit. End of. You do not need to go out and buy a load of books on dream interpretation or dream encyclopaedias. In fact I urge you not to, particularly if you are just starting out on this epic and wondrous journey. Some of them are confusing and they could potentially lead you astray or round in circles. Of course I realise that there is an implicit irony in my adding to this cacophony, but I hope I will lead you back to the main event: your personal relationship with God and your training manual: the Bible. If you want to turf this here and now and just swot the dreams in the Bible this minute, feel free. The value in this book is that hopefully I will communicate what to focus on, what to avoid and some pitfalls I've learned given I've pilgrimed this road 'afore you.' You may be further along this road than me. I don't like to be presumptuous, but we all journey this eternal road together as pilgrims passing through, and we all learn from each other, so let's crack on together, staffs aloft.

A Note for people who might not believe in God

I've written this book for Christians and non Christians alike, given God gives dreams to believers and non believers, and clearly all of humanity dreams. However, if you are a non believer, you may find some of the content peculiar or unusual, but I believe God speaks to all of us through dreams. When I refer to God, however, I mean God the Father, God the Son—Jesus—and God the Holy Spirit, aka The Trinity, or the triune God; the Judeo Christian God. I believe all aspects of God are God, so Jesus is God to me, as is the Holy Spirit - the part of God we engage with on the earth now that Jesus has returned to heaven. I tend to refer to Christians as 'believers' as in 'followers of Jesus,' or believers in the gospel that Jesus preached,' as in the New Testament teachings of Christ, given the term Christian is so loaded and so many who use the term don't follow Christ. They might call themselves Christian in a cultural way for example, but they may not be actual followers of Christ. If you are not a Christian, or a 'believer,' it is important to know that the Bible is a book of prophecy. By example, the New Testament events were prophesied in the Old Testament - this is key - given if the Old Testament did not reveal who Jesus was, in hundreds of prophecies, Jesus could have just been making himself up all along. In other words, He could not have been a conman with a Messiah complex rather than the God He is revealed through the prophecies to be. If you are interested in reading more about the truth regarding the historical Jesus and the chances of the Old Testament prophecies proving the veracity of the birth, death and resurrection of Jesus, please attend an Alpha course somewhere. I found the 'proof of Jesus' aspects of the Alpha course compelling. Also see the scholarly works of Hugh Ross and Big Bang Cosmology. In terms of the Old Testament foretelling the new, please see the writings of the famed mathematician, Professor Peter Stoner, chairman of the mathematics and astronomy departments at Pasadena City College until 1953, and then chairman of the science division at Westmont College in Santa Barbara, California. The chances of anyone fulfilling the over 300 prophecies as were written in the Bible about Jesus' birth and life, that were written between 500 and 1000 years before Jesus was even born is a trillion, trillion, trillion, trillion, trillion, trillion, trillion, trillion, trillion, trillion, trillion, trillion, trillion![1] And Jesus had to fulfil every single one, or He was not the Messiah at all but a madman - as first brilliantly pointed out by the author and apologist, C.S Lewis. The probability that someone could fulfil just eight of these new testament prophecies about Jesus, is one in 100,000,000,000,000,000.[2] There is no way one man could have fulfilled all 8 of these prophecies unless God was making it happen. Stoner's book is called *Evidence That Demands a Verdict*. Personally, and despite the dreams and visions I had had, I needed to know of God logically, with my mind, as well as spiritually, with my spirit, before I surrendered to a life of following Jesus, (by giving my life to Him in exchange for His giving His life for me). I was a tough nut to crack but God was merciful to me due to the defence mechanisms I had built up over the years to survive. For more on this divine exchange, please

---

[1] https://www.icsv.at/one-chance-in-a-trillion-trillion-trillion-trillion-trillion-trillion-trillion-trillion-trillion-trillion-trillion-trillion

[2] https://nickcady.org/2020/02/18/the-statistical-probability-of-jesus-fulfilling-the-messianic-prophecies/

read the Gospel accounts of Jesus, in Matthew, Mark, Luke and John in the Bible. Please buy yourself a Bible and read it. It really is the best book you will ever purchase and is the world's best selling book of all time[3] for good reason. Next in line is 'Quotations from Chairman Mao Tse-Tung'—900 million, The Quran—at least 800 million, then 'Xinhua Zidian'—567 million and then a work of literature, 'Don Quixote'—at least 500 million. Tolkien has sold 100 million copies of *The Hobbit*.[4] For those of you that don't already know this, Tolkien was a Philologist, a writer, a Christian and a contemporary and friend of C.S Lewis who wrote *The Lion the Witch and the Wardrobe* amongst other classics. A singular Christian thinker and apologist, Lewis has written many brilliant works of Christian apologetics too. The only other book that comes remotely close in my opinion is the complete works of Shakespeare. Shakespeare was well versed in the verses as it were. In a book published by Oxford University Press, called *Shakespeare and the Bible*, the author, Stephen Marx, suggests that the Bible inspired Shakespeare's uses of myth, history, comedy, and tragedy, his techniques of staging, and his ways of characterising of rulers, magicians and teachers in the image of the Bible's multifaceted God. Regardless of the version used, there are roughly 1,350 total identifiable instances where Shakespeare references or quotes directly

---

[3] https://www.guinnessworldrecords.com/world-records/best-selling-book-of-non-fiction

[4] https://www.deseret.com/2023/12/22/24011218/bestselling-individual-books-of-all-time/

from the Geneva Bible found throughout his plays[5]. The Bible and the works of Shakespeare are the foundation stones of English culture, and the Bible was a major source of Shakespeare's allusions and references given the Bible was the text most available to people in early modern England. The Bible is a powerful book. In 1525, William Tyndale risked his life to translate the Bible from Greek into plain English for common folk to read. He would be martyred in 1536 for making the New Testament available to all. Indeed, he was in the process of translating the Old Testament when he was killed. Prior to this the Bible was only available to be read in churches by priests in Latin—the Latin version translated over a thousand years prior by the catholic monk Jerome, who died in 420. People have been burned at the stake or martyred in various ways for the Bible to be made freely available to you and I. Tyndale coined new phrases, metaphors and indeed grammar, to illustrate the Greek and Hebrew as he translated it into plain English and in so doing venerated an entire language. Thank God for Tyndale and for subsequent Bible translators; the explosive power of the word of God can now be heard articulated in our mother tongue—and many others in translation—a tongue made more lucid by Tyndale's Bible and the influence it had on our language as the primary text. It is of course the primary text for dream interpretation too, which is why I am waxing lyrically about it now. Personally, I have no doubt that the Bible is a life changing book, particularly when the reader is engaged with and animated by the power of God through the Holy

---

[5] The Bard and The Word: the influence of the Bible on the writings of William Shakespeare, Emily Gray, May 2018, University of Tennesse, at Chattanooga; https://scholar.utc.edu/cgi/viewcontent.cgi?article=1140&context=honors-theses

Spirit. If you follow its instructions, you will be transformed by it. It's the maker's manual!

The big questions are: Who am I? Why am I here? What should I be doing? Jesus answers them all. I've done the research and have discovered for myself that it's all true. I've studied the world religions and practised numerology and astrology (repented; dealt with) meditated and cogitated and travelled the world and traversed the pages of books, searching for answers. Don't wait a single moment longer for true confidence, faith, joy and the meaning of life. There is one book and one book only that answers all the questions and proves itself, just as Jesus proves Himself: the Bible. It's essential that we all look into this. It is not enough to decide whether you want to believe or not. We don't get to decide. We get to accept or not—this is free will, but there are always consequences for actions. If you're not convinced, do the research and look at science and history around creation and Jesus—neither disciplines are incompatible with belief in Christ. Then invite Jesus into your life. Or do so now to test the theory: Apologise for going your own way and thinking you are your own God and ask him to forgive you for any wrong doing and ask Him to lead you from now on. And get a Bible. The Bible is the instruction manual for all aspects of life. How do you think we get the phrase 'to know someone in a biblical way.' Amongst many informative phrases from the Bible to Shakespeare. I use a capital 'H' for 'himself' or 'him', when referring to God or aspects of God—Jesus/the Holy Spirit, (the part of God that is available to all who accept Jesus as the son of God and invite Him into their lives) or even the Holy Ghost as he's sometimes known. These past two names still partly do my head in as they are a bit woo woo, or ghosty, but given I can't come up with an alternative here, and even if I did it would likely confuse matters. After all, I'm already asking you to take it on board that God is Father, son and Holy Ghost, which becomes completely logical when you receive the revelation of who God is, but seems downright batty to folks who don't believe in God. If you remain unconvinced about God I challenge you to think atheism through again from beginning to the end, not leaving out how the universe operates and the notion of free will, I suggest CS. Lewis again for more on this: *Mere Christianity* is a good place to start. He is a far greater boffin than me on theology and the universe and everything. One last but very important point. Just as God exists so does the enemy of God, the devil or satan who wars against creation and humanity—the ones in His image, for relationship with Him. Satan seeks to influence people whether they are awake or asleep, so we need to be fully plugged into the correct sources—God and the Bible—to make sure we do not become influenced by an ungodly source. If you happen to be reading this and don't believe in God yet, just suspend your disbelief for now if you are curious about dreams, but I will be using the Bible and my own experience to explain dreams and how to decode them. Now you know where I stand. On the rock, basically. And I don't mean Dwayne, The Rock.

In summary, God has spoken to humankind across the ages through dreams, visions, poetry and song, to say nothing of His glorious painterly displays of creativity and joy all over the earth and the cosmos. He delights in the creation of you—only He could have thought you up, and He adores you so much that as the Bible puts it, even the hairs on your head are numbered— as well as your days—and nights, so make good use of them as you will spend roughly a third of your life sleeping and thus many hours dreaming, and for good purpose as you will see. Incidentally, there is lots of information on the internet on sleep and dreams if you fancy doing some research. From what I can tell, these experts have not looked at the Bible record of dreams. If they did, it might help them with their research, but at lease they are studying and paying attention to them, unlike many believers! So hats off to them and thinking caps on for the rest of us! I would also like to say this to you: God is not religious. People are. This is not a 'religious' book but it does use the Bible as the primary text for interpreting dreams. I don't recommend any other book or manual or guide for dream interpretation. Instead of the word 'Christian,' I prefer the word 'believer' or 'follower of Jesus' for myself as in the UK where I currently live, Christianity is generally frowned upon in the culture and Christians are associated with the worst crimes of the churches, many of which are corrupt in their structures, power bases and their peddling of wares and excesses with money. Many Christians do profoundly good works and model Christ well in community, and thank God for those who officiate at Christenings, weddings and funerals, so I don't want to throw the baby out with the bathwater here, but it is my personal belief that were Jesus here, he wouldn't be parked off in a pew or gaping at some Christian guru, he'd be out there in the places that people congregated, just as he was in His day. I am not against tradition and even ritual, nor modern Christian teachers and preachers who are not self serving, but how the Christian Church has veered so far off the path that is modelled by Jesus Christ and the disciples is beyond me, and has been from day one of my becoming a believer, some 24 years ago. I understand that you might find the word 'believer' a tricky construct as people can believe in all manner of things from Aliens abducting Elvis to red skies at night to only eating fish on a Friday or going to church on Sundays, but given you know the context, my explanation should suffice. Jesus ushered in and modelled a kingdom that is one based on grace (freedom and free gifts) and not works. Jesus was the personification of God the Father and he demonstrated the all encompassing love of the father by sacrificially going to the cross as a scapegoat for humanities' sins. If this sounds far out, there is more on this in the Bible and I encourage you to study it for yourself. Suffice to say, I will use the term 'God' to refer to God the Father, God the Son (Jesus) and God the Holy Spirit (the power of God available to believers in order to operate in this day as He did on the earth 2000+ years ago). True dream interpretation comes from the God of the Bible, and the word of God.

Chapter 1. The Vital Importance of Dreams to the Body of Christ

"he said, "Listen to my words: "When there is a prophet among you, I, the LORD, reveal myself to them in visions, I speak to them in dreams."
Numbers 12:6

It was Christmas 2022. On my birthday, I was in a swimming pool in Australia chatting (praying) to God and asking about the season ahead. In response to my request for a birthday gift, (if you don't ask you don't receive!) God responded: "You have the mind of Christ." Before you leap to the conclusion that I have a Messiah Complex, this is a biblical gift and what it means is that we all, if we are 'in Christ' through belief in Him, have access to His mind (1 Corinthians 2:16). Which means we have access to the mind that created the universe as well as to the wisdom of the ages, never mind the sages. This is, frankly, mind boggling, and remains an abstract concept to many. He then went on to show me that in the seasons to come, the world would be in great turmoil—I saw kingdoms rising and falling—war and chaos—and that the commodity that people would need above all else, was wisdom. The wisdom that comes through God via the Holy Spirit. Dreams and visions are a vital way that God communicates with us. Why would any of us humans ever want to miss out on this form of wisdom? Especially since dreams are so lavishly packaged and delivered to you each morning like sweet fresh bread with a glorious helping of French apricot reserve and cold salted butter? Just the way you, or I, like it! (Most dreams are very personal, and most of them are for you.)

It is amazing to me how many believers will slavishly follow certain preachers or teachers but are not true students of the Bible themselves. When one reads the book of Acts, we can hear the genius of Paul made plain to us across the millennia just as if he was speaking to us from a prison where he was making requests by letter to his believing brothers—*Can someone send me my cloak?* "When you come, bring the cloak that I left with Carpus at Troas, and my scrolls, especially the parchments," (2 Timothy 4:13). It is a most precious and holy thing to own and be able to study the Bible, yet so many take it for granted and graze on comparative guff instead. Idiomatic references from both the Bible and Shakespeare glimmer like stars in the English language yet increasingly the Bible is dismissed in our culture, despite the fact that it is our greatest source of wisdom and knowledge; and our western democracies and our rule of law are biblically based: I refer to English Law and the American Constitution. Even the works of Shakespeare are under threat in UK syllabuses and may well be whitewashed from whiteboards at a school near you soon. The modern roots of our individual rights and freedoms in the Western world are found in Christianity and the notion that we answer to a higher law—God's moral superiority. This is biblically found and based. Watching human liberty, rights and freedom erode, (and classic works of literature being ransacked by jittery publishers to make them more more palatable for reactive modern audiences) as state power becomes increasingly pervasive, as is the case in modern Britain, is not progressive, rather it is a return to the past where the individual did not matter as much as an ideology; we see the outworking of this in communism or in countries where fundamentalism rules through arbitrary power. The recognition by law of the intrinsic value of each human being did not exist in ancient times, man was a cog in a machine, and the machine belonged to whomever wielded state or empirical power—such as the Roman Empire, or more recently, the Nazis in Germany's former fascist state. We see the same in fundamentalist religious regimes, such as that of Iran. But let us not make the mistake that our countries are immune to the excesses we observe in 'other' nations. Terrifyingly state control, disguised as compassion and in cahoots with large sectors of the population is taking place in the UK as I write and is rapidly increasing. I say all this to demonstrate the angle this book is taking as far as resources and sources of revelation go. I use the Bible for all aspects of life and for dream interpretation: this is the immutable law that we can trust, laid down for us by the God from whom morality, ethics and infinite wisdom stems. The God who made heaven and earth speaks to people through dreams and visions as He did to the Hebrews, Romans, Babylonians and Egyptians of ancient times—who took the wisdom of dreams far more seriously than many of us modern agers do, though there is no less need for wisdom from the maker of all, particularly given the state of the world today. Where has human wisdom got us? But as we see through the Bible in history, it is human beings listening to God through dreams and visions that has changed the course of history. Pictures or visions are the language of heaven and of the spirit. Human beings are body, mind & emotions or soul, but also spirit, and our spirits are eternal—this visionary language is the language of the eternal. Best to learn it, pronto, if you haven't already. And you can!

In Proverbs 29:18 we are told that, "Where there is no revelation, people cast off restraint; but blessed is the one who heeds wisdom's instruction." It is vital that we are able to hear from God. In my opinion, the church (as in, the people of God; it doesn't really matter where you hang out, as long as you do) has become severely weakened or has not matured effectively, because people cannot interpret dreams and visions, nor can many adequately or comprehensively, discern the voice of God. There are other issues as well, such as following patterns laid down by culture and tradition, rather than the Kingdom of God, but that is for another book! If we cannot correctly hear from God, who might we be hearing from given there are two other sources of guidance, neither of them satisfactory? God communicates with each one of us uniquely and personally through dreams. They are His personal parables to us. Imagine having Jesus sit down with you under a tree on a hillside and tell you a story crafted just for you? Well, I'm here to say He does just that through the Holy Spirit via dreams and visions. If you don't comprehend the meaning of your dreams straight away then you're in good company. When Jesus told the disciples parables, they were baffled and sought Him out for the meaning. We need to do the same ourselves today after we have had a dream. It's not rocket science, it's a case of "Seek and you will find, knock and the door will be opened to you," (Matthew 7:7). Jesus is the door of revelation and truth. He is the revealed word of God as foretold in the Old Testament of the Bible. He visits every day with messages, whether we remember or discern them or not, and He is waiting to communicate with you, his beloved child whom He longs to intimately converse with. "What is mankind that you make so much of them, that you give them so much attention, *that you examine them every morning* and test them every moment?" Job 7;17–18. Why would we want to miss this opportunity to hear from Him? Particularly since hearing from God can be life saving and life altering as we shall see. We are living in an era where people are increasingly desperate to hear the wisdom of God and to understand what dreams and visions mean. As the days get darker and the nights draw in, people will become increasingly desperate to hear from the correct source, from the throne of God Himself. The Bible—the objective *logos* word of God, coupled with the *rhema* word of God—the revealed, subjective revelation that God gives through the Holy Spirit is the only true way of learning dreams and these are the only two resources you need. The Holy Spirit of God, the *paraclete* is the only helper you need to quicken revelation to you and help you unlock the code of your dream which leads to the interpretation. I have been keeping journals of dreams and visions for decades. I have learnt what they all mean through this process, and I have learnt to rely on these two sources only. It is vital that believers hear the voice of God for themselves, so that we are not subject to human error, neither do we want to come into agreement with ungodly forces and strategies. By keeping a journal, I also track where and how my dreams and visions have come to pass and take note of where I might have gone wrong in order to improve. This has taken many years and I continue to learn, but perhaps it will be faster for you. I hope and pray it is, given the worldwide body of believers needs to be fit, well and unified (not uniform—how dull) for service. The Christian journey is like a relay race in which we seize the baton from those that have gone before us and then we run our own bit of the race as well as we can do, before passing the baton on! The Bible tells us that people are dying through lack of knowledge: "my people are destroyed from lack of knowledge. Because you have rejected knowledge, I also reject you as my priests; because you have ignored the law of your God, I also will ignore your children." (Hosea 4:6). Strong warning there not to 'ignore the law'. The law being referred to there is the Hebrew Scriptures, or Old Testament. I honestly believe that sometimes He gives us the knowledge to prevent us from dying through dreams. My own life bears this out and you can read about this later in this book.

Chapter 2. How God Speaks through Dreams

"For God does speak—now one way, now another—
though no one perceives it."
Job 33:14

I go to bed every night, hoping and praying for a dream. It never fails to thrill me that God speaks through dreams. I'm usually gutted if I wake and can't remember a dream, or only get snatches of it, like a single, disappointing bite of a cake when I want to scarf the whole thing down with lashings of coffee and conversation with God. During the third of life I have spent sleeping, or attempting to (I'm not lazy, it's the same for all of us), He has warned me, outlined my calling, healed me, corrected me and joked with me through dreams. Over the 24 years that I have been interpreting dreams and visions, for myself and for many others around the world, I have found that this is the purest source of revelation from God outside of the Bible. When we sleep, God can speak to us 'face to face' as it were. Not as in sitting across from a friend in a coffee shop, but actually in an even more unadulterated way, or if you like, with no filter—but in an absolutely good way! Here is our opportunity to walk with God in the cool of the day, or in the twilight world of a garden of Eden, where daily distractions cannot intrude and where we can give Him our full attention. When we sleep God is able to speak directly to our spirit man (or woman). Dreams and visions can take on many types, from single snapshots or 'stills' to rapidly moving scenes as in a movie. It is up to us to unpack the meaning or hidden message through the symbolism of the dream coding and apply it to its setting and the context of our lives. God is creating the dream coding as we dream, but he has hardwired us to understand His visual coding—to learn dream coding. When we sleep, our natural man or our soul man is not operating or in control and this is very key. A dream is like a system override where God bypasses our usual conscious processing or our usual preoccupations to commune directly with our spirits. "While you dream, some parts of your brain are more active than others. Regions involved in sensory processing, memory, and emotion fire off lots of messages, while the parts responsible for logic and reasoning quiet down" (brainfacts.org). As King Solomon put it: "I slept but my heart (spirit) was awake." Dreams are creative, they require interaction between the dream giver and the dream receiver in order to decode them, and then to apply them to our life circumstances, or for them to come into being: like a writer of a book and a reader thereof. This requires choice. It is an act of the will of the person receiving the dream. God, who made you, does not force His will upon you. Rather, He gives you free will. God communes with our spirit man as we sleep and the message is transferred to our minds which is our centre for remembering and decoding— making sense of the dream code. This is also the centre of our imaginations where we 'make' images or pictures, the place of internal vision. We all have this visual making capability in our minds and neuroscientists explain how this works if you would like to do a study on it. Basically, if I ask you to visualise a pink elephant you can project that through your 'minds eye.' As you sleep your spirit projects what God has imparted from His spirit to yours and these are fed to the visual centres in our brains for processing. As believers it is our sacred task to keep our minds renewed by the 'washing of the word' of God through reading the Bible and being transformed by it, and remaining unpolluted by imagery being transmitted to us by the world and from ungodly sources so that these images are not recalled and projected during sleep. In the Bible this is called having your mind renewed: "Do not conform to the pattern of this world, but be transformed by the renewing of your mind. Then you will be able to test and approve what God's will is—his good, pleasing and perfect will." (Romans 12:2). Mind renewal through the Bible is like having your brain 'debugged' from the rubbish that world culture often transmits, as well as other, ungodly sources. We need to be resolute about what we allow into us and around us. King David said: "I will not look with approval on anything that is vile. I hate what faithless people do; I will have no part in it," (Psalm 101:3). Jesus warns us that we can become darkened in our understanding if we do not watch ourselves and what we watch: "The eye is the lamp of the body. If your eyes are healthy, your whole body will be full of light," (Matthew 6:22). Conversely if you become darkened from ungodly sources, your whole understanding will become darkened, and this is how you will operate—in tandem with the enemy: As Paul warns: "They are darkened in their understanding and separated from the life of God because of the ignorance that is in them due to the hardening of their hearts," (Ephesians 4:18). You can unknowingly become separated from God and operate from an ungodly realm, thinking your revelation is from God—this is the domain of false revelation or the counterfeit. More on that later in this book.

I believe information comes to us in dreams and visions from three sources—the third heaven where God resides as outlined in the Bible (revelation); the second heaven, which is the demonic realm; and the first heaven—earth. From the second realm, satan can project dark thoughts and visual information to our minds. The enemy of our souls gains access to our minds through breaches in unhealed souls. He cannot create dreams nor communicate spirit to spirit as God can, but he can use our highly reflective, troubled or unhealed souls as a screen to project false information to our minds—which is why healing, deliverance and the process of mind renewal are imperatives for believers. For example, if you are a man suffering from lust, he may project a pornographic dream onto the screen of your soul in order to make you feel more guilty. His *modus operandi* is to get you to focus on him and not God, and to make you feel ashamed and worthless. This has been his motivation since the garden. Witches, tarot readers and psychics receive their revelation from the second realm where 'watcher spirits' or demons that watch people reside. This is how a psychic or medium can tell a person that Great Aunt Bertha was wearing purple shoes, pink knickers and a jade brooch when she died. They can also channel and mimic the voices of deceased family members and so on. The Bible is very clear that such practises are evil and not of God and should not be tampered with. They open a door to evil in a person's life. Believers who have previously tampered with the dark realm by going to psychics or playing the ouija board and the like will need to seek forgiveness from God and be cleansed from this and in some cases delivered from opening themselves up to demons or demonic influence. If believers have not 'closed the door' to the second heaven they can still operate out of this realm or operate in a mixture of true and false revelation which is also dangerous however unwittingly. More on this tricksy mix later in this book. As we sleep, transmissions coloured by our own imaginations, preoccupations or anxieties can arise from our subconscious to our conscious minds as we process information. These types of dreams can be revealing and instructive as they hold up a mirror to our hearts and minds but are not necessarily direct messages from God with directives or warnings.

Nightmares are often a sign that you are healing from trauma or a heart issue that God wants to release you from, particularly if a nightmare recurs. Traumatic or hurtful experiences can become deeply buried in us in order for us to cope. Nightmares can reveal what is happening in the demonic realm and give strategy and revelation as to how to pray to frustrate satanic plans for believers. Do not be quick to dismiss a dream that might have freaky elements like discovering old bones or people who have passed for instance, this can be God revealing that there are elements to do with the past that need dealing with. Some 'dark' dreams are from God as we see with Abram's dream: "As the sun was setting, Abram fell into a deep sleep, and a thick and dreadful darkness came over him," (Genesis 15:12). Via the dream, the slavery of Abram's descendants in Egypt, their eventual exodus, and their conquest of the sinful nations of Canaan is foretold. God likely communicated this way as the significance of the dream would have been too fearful or profound for Abram to grasp at that point in time. God will scare you to 'wake you up' in order to deliver a point that you are not getting by other means. Sometimes the dream will be 'sealed' for a future date, when you are ready to receive it. Dreams from God have a logical, clear message however weird they might seem before they are decoded. Sometimes a nightmare can reveal an area that we need to be delivered from. Sexual dreams can reveal that we need to be delivered from a spirit of lust for example, or you can be being harassed by an impure spirit if your soul is not yet healed or transformed in this area. Job 33, 16–19 says (my comments are in brackets), "Then He opens the ears of men, And *seals* their instruction, That He may turn man aside from his conduct, (warns us against sinful conduct) And keep man from pride, He keeps back his soul from the pit, (saves our lives) And his life from passing over into Sheol (hell), Man is also chastened with pain on his bed (if you don't listen to God you might get sick!), And with unceasing complaint in his bones," (or arthritic—especially if you get bitter—as 'bitterness dries up the bones'—"A cheerful heart is good medicine, but a crushed spirit dries up the bones," (Proverbs 17:22)). God, in His mercy, sometimes seals His instruction to our minds but our spirits receive the impartation as even when our minds sleep our spirits are awake to God's instructions: "I slept but my heart (spirit – sic) was awake. Listen! My beloved is knocking: "Open to me, my sister, my darling, my dove, my flawless one. My head is drenched with dew, my hair with the dampness of the night." (Song of Solomon 5:2).

There is much in the Bible about treasure, and seeking it out, given treasure and precious jewels are often used as analogies and symbols for the kingdom of God. It says in Proverbs 25:2 that "it is the glory of God to conceal a matter; to search out a matter (here one could usefully, but not implicitly, insert the word 'dream') is the glory of kings.". The language of heaven is visual treasure which is why there is so much poetry, parable and symbolism in the Bible. Consider a dream an invitation into God's heart, an invitation to dream with Him. I've heard dreams described as God's love letters, but this feels a bit dream 'lite,' or Rom-Com. There are thrillers, action movies and dramas galore in the dream canon, but most certainly they are transmitted with love and for love and out of love, from God to you as the previous quotation from the Song of Solomon illustrates. You have the potential to discover God's heart for you through your dreams. God is a poet and all the prophecy in the Bible is poetic. The visual language of poetry is symbol and metaphor as is the language of the Bible and of God. You really have been hard wired by the master programmer to understand this language and you can. All it takes is some patience, a manual (Bible) and a teacher (Jesus – through the Holy Spirit) and a notebook and pen - dream journal. You wouldn't go to school without any of these three bits of equipment, right? If you are unschooled in dreams, now is your chance to get cracking.

Sometimes dreamers and visionaries are dismissed as mystics and madmen. Dreams and visions are indeed mystical and mystics have dreams and visions but we can all experience and benefit from this mystical realm. People are often sceptical of the provenance of dreams, and often rightly so. The bible warns us to 'test the spirits, to see whether they are from God,' (1 John: 4). The Oxford Dictionary defines 'mystical' as "having spiritual powers or qualities that are difficult to understand or explain." The word is derived from the noun 'mystic'—'a person who uses prayer and meditation to try to become united with God or to understand important things that are beyond human understanding.' I would describe myself as a mystic, but this needs to be placed in context so that you do not get the wrong impression and form the opinion that I am a nutter. When you become a believer, or follower of Jesus and accept the Holy Spirit into your life as your counsellor, teacher and guide, certain gifts that you are born with are activated by the power of the Holy Spirit who has come to reside in you once you have accepted Jesus into your life. The gifts of the Holy Spirit are listed in 1 Corinthians 12: 7–11. In the ancient sense, I am a mystic or visionary—in life and in the spirit. Spiritually speaking, I function as a member of the *ekklesia (the ekklesia* is the gathering of the believers in a place or situation; not necessarily in a church building; the members who make up 'the body of Christ' which is symbolic of the *ekklesia)*. In the prophetic lineage of the biblical seers, and the Celtic believers, but I also interpret dreams across the board as it were. Daniel and Joseph were seers who had the spiritual gift of discernment as did the apostles Paul, Peter and John for instance—all of whom were seers as well. The Bible can be a little confusing on its definitions of prophets and I don't pretend to be a student of Aramaic, Hebrew or Greek, so have not done an exhaustive study on prophetic function but my definition of a seer prophet is 'one who sees.' One who sees into all the realms, with both internal and external eyes; one who has heavenly visitations; and one who can see 'behind the scenes,' where God gives knowledge about a corporate situation that is going that most people cannot see. Seers can also see into the caverns of people's hearts when God reveals information for His purposes or outcomes to be established: Samuel answered Saul and said, "I am the seer [ra'ah]. Go up before me to the high place, for you shall eat with me today; tomorrow I will let you go and will tell you all that is in your heart." (1 Samuel 9:19). God reveals information to seers that they could not have otherwise known (which comes to pass: this cannot be said unless there is documented proof and seers and interpreters should be able to produce the fruit of their ministries to inspection; which is why it is important to document and show how what is seen has come to pass). God reveals secrets to his prophets: "Surely the Lord God does nothing, unless He reveals His secret to His servants the prophets." (Amos 3:7). Incidentally, Amos was a seer with no prophetic background when God called him into His service. He must have been the one who He felt He could trust. God will look for one that He can 'send.' From this we surmise God given capability being activated in Amos, but also a willingness to engage with God. he was called by God after a vision. Peter discerned that Ananias and Saphira had both lied to the Holy Spirit. "But Peter said, "Ananias, why has Satan filled your heart to lie to the Holy Spirit and to keep back for yourself part of the proceeds of the land? While it remained unsold, did it not remain your own? And after it was sold, was it not at your disposal? Why is it that you have contrived this deed in your heart? You have not lied to man but to God." (Acts 5, 3–5). It is important to see that lies of all kinds are never 'white' or right. When we lie, we lie to God and in this case, the couple dropped down dead.

Personally, I see scriptural language like a movie playing out in my head when I am talking to people if God is trying to alert me to pray or otherwise hep in a particular situation. Before you draw the conclusion that I have an Elijah or Daniel complex as in the psychotic context of a Messiah complex, I hasten to explain: I have had some of the experiences that biblical prophets had in terms of dreams and visions —I am not putting myself on the same level as them, only that I identify with some of their experiences. I am a normal flawed human being in the process of Holy Spirit sanctification with weaknesses being transformed into strengths by engagement with the Holy Spirit, and do not always get things right, but I always try to make things right, or learn what is right. The Bible calls this state of being 'righteousness' or being in right standing with God. Believers are not perfect, but they do need to be sincere in their efforts to follow Christ's example. Elijah's visions can be read in the book of Kings in the Bible. His experiences were 'far out' in the truest sense of the phrase. He had open visions, in that the supernatural, or spiritual visions that he saw, he saw with his spiritual eyes—in internal visions or 'pictures' seen in the spirit or through 'the mind's eye' as well as through his natural eyes—like we see people generally, for example. Unless you are suffering from shell shock or other forms of hallucination, there are two ways of seeing: with your natural eyes and with your spiritual eyes. I don't need to explain how you see in the

37

natural, you do that every day. People are made of body, soul and spirit. Your body and soul–mind, will and emotions are with you 24/7. But you also have a spirit, and that spirit also operates with mind, will and emotions. If this sounds bonkers, consider the stories of people who have 'died' on the operating table. They often describe being above their bodies and looking down at the commotion below. Then there is the 'tunnel of light experience,' and believers in Jesus often describe a meeting with Him or with members of their families who have gone home before them when they are about to pass on. Clearly their body is still on the operating table because when they return or are sent back, their time is not yet up, so they return to their bodies. In other words, the spirit, that is usually resident in the body, is capable of operating without the body, and as it does so, it does as a thinking, sentient being. God Himself is three in one: Father, Son and Holy Spirit. If you can appreciate that God is three people in one, you can appreciate that you are two people in one, for as long as you are physically on the earth at any rate. The Bible says that "to be absent from the body is to be present with the Lord," which means that when we are not in the body, we are in the realm of God. This is a mystery, but one that I hope I have just explained. If you do not believe this, I hope you will suspend your disbelief until you have read further. When you are asleep then, God, through the Holy Spirit, can commune directly with your spirit. In other words, God can override your body, mind, will and emotions and speak directly to your spirit. What you do with the messages God sends, is entirely up to you. Here is your opportunity to exercise your own free will. If however, God is communicating direction for your life, surely it is best to sit up and listen? We can all have these 'mystical' experiences, and we do, thus we can all be 'mystics,' it's not weird. We just don't always recognise them as such. God who is shrouded in mystery, nevertheless makes himself known to us during the night through dreams, and by visions that usually come by day. If you open yourself up to dreams you will likely start having more visions as well. Revelation upon revelation!

Chapter 3. What are Dreams and Visions Exactly?

A vision can be a static picture or image, seen with your internal eyes or with your external eyes. It can also be a moving sequence of events seen with either your internal or external eyes. A dream is also a moving sequence of events, with scenes like that of a film, which take place in the darkroom of your mind at night, but you can receive daydreams too, when you 'drift off' and are not quite asleep nor awake. All of these ways of receiving images can be spiritual. To say 'it was just my imagination,' which it can be, is to potentially dismiss the sacred along with the profane, like throwing a lottery ticket away accidentally or without properly perceiving the numbers. Your mind (imagination) and soul can project pictures too, but the ones that come 'unbidden' when you are not necessarily thinking along those lines can very likely be from God. Satan, agent of evil and master God impersonator can do this too, so you need to examine the fruit of the dream or vision. As Jesus said in Matthew 7:16 "By their fruit you will recognise them. Do people pick grapes from thorn bushes, or figs from thistles?" God speaks according to His character and the devil, his. If the vision or 'dream' resonates with the Bible and your spirit, it is probably God speaking to you. If not, seek wise counsel from your circle of trusted believers or dismiss summarily. Satan tries to transmit false information or 'false dreams' to us in the twilight of sleeping and waking, but these are not 'true dreams,' from God. God convicts in His kindness, but the enemy condemns.

Approximately one third of the Bible shows people interacting with God through dreams and visions[6]. Dreams are variously described in the bible as 'night visions or visions of the night.' If given by God's spirit, they are birthed in the spirit, transmitted to the mind in the form of images or symbols, and decoded with the skill of the dreamer, along with the hand of the artist Himself—the Holy Spirit. (if originating from Him). Visions are described as 'waking dreams' see Numbers 24:4. As with visions, dreams can arise from the natural mind or the imagination. God commonly used dreams and visions to communicate with people in the Bible as He does today, though astonishingly, people seem less interested in this divine form of communication these days. In the Old Testament, visions were common and when they dissipated due to a lack of prophets (1 Samuel 3:1), or the disobedience of God's people, (1 Samuel 28:6), the people suffered for the lack of this communication, and I reiterate, we, the church, suffer for the lack of taking our dreams seriously today. "Indeed God speaks once, or twice, yet no one notices it" (Job 33 14). God is willing to give us fresh manna from heaven each morning, yet we look to the past or to the future for more when we could have more now! God still speaks through prophets today, and seer prophets still dream dreams and see visions, internally and externally. This is one of the most exciting ways that the kingdom of heaven invades earth and it is available to all.

---

[6] Laurie-Ann Zachar, December 1998 edition of Fellowship Magazine

Example of a vision that is like a snapshot, or a still image

When training him to see in the spirit or with his spiritual eyes, God asked Jeremiah what he could *see.* Jeremiah *saw* an almond branch: "The word of the LORD came to me: "What do you see, Jeremiah?" "I see the branch of an almond tree," I replied," (Jeremiah 1:11). Jeremiah *saw* the word of the Lord (God). This is how God speaks, in words and symbols projected into our 'mind's eye.'

In Amos 8:1, God shows Amos a static vision of basket of fruit. Amos could see it, presumably with his spiritual eyes. God spoke with Amos about the picture and explained what it meant: "This is what the Sovereign Lord showed me: a basket of ripe fruit. "What do you see, Amos?" he asked.
"A basket of ripe fruit," I answered.
Then the Lord said to me, "The time is ripe for my people Israel; I will spare them no longer,"" God gives the meaning of the symbols in the static vision. The basket of fruit is symbolic of time being up for the people of Israel.

Example of a vision in sequence, like a film

Amos sees a vision of fire sweeping over the crops and destroying them. He is also shown a vision of locusts swarming and destroying the crops in Amos 7:1. In both of these visions, there is action and movement, like moving pictures, in a film. He later shows him a plumb line to symbolise his righteousness in the coming judgement by fire.

Example of a moving image with sound

Joel had a vision of an army of locusts in Joel 2:1–11, in which he describes action and sound: "They have the appearance of horses; they gallop along like cavalry. With a noise like that of chariots they leap over the mountaintops, like a crackling fire consuming stubble, like a mighty army drawn up for battle." The repeated similes: 'like'—one symbol illustrating another, highlight the vivid, moving flashes of action, like a shutter opening and closing. The action unfolds in highly poetic and visual language.

Trances

Peter has a vision where a sheet containing all sorts of unclean animals is let down in front of him. God tells him to "kill and eat." Here Peter could interact with the vision. When Peter refused to eat because the animals were 'unclean' in Jewish culture, God rebuked him for calling things unclean that God does not call unclean. This vision was repeated three times. Peter was in a trance when he had this vision (Acts 10:10). His physical body may not have been engaged, but in his spirit, he was interacting with the vision. If God says something to you three times, as in three scenes in a dream or three consecutive dreams, sit up and take heed! These things will surely come to pass. In this case, God was showing how Gentiles as well as Jews are welcome in the kingdom of God. You can thank God for this vision whether you are a Jew or a Gentile believer given God had set Peter and the Godly Roman Centurion Cornelius up for an encounter: He arranged for an angel to tell Cornelius, that Peter would be arriving to see him. Cornelius was the first non Jew or Gentile to be baptised into the *ekklesia* of Christ. We follow in his lineage. What a privilege. You can read the whole story that begins with a visitation and a trance and ends with the Holy Spirit coming to the Gentiles in Acts 10. It's action packed, and it's our story too!

Open Visions

In open visions you can hear, see, taste, feel and smell the things that are happening around you. Heaven invades earth and you see it. In some cases, some senses (usually sight and hearing) operate but others do not. Ezekiel had open visions: "In my thirtieth year, in the fourth month on the fifth day, while I was among the exiles by the Kebar River, the heavens were opened and I saw visions of God." (Ezekiel 1:1). To say that Ezekiel's visions were mind blowing is an understatement. He gives Daniel and St John a run for their money. There is sometimes a crossover between the visual episodes we experience. The words 'dreams' and 'visions' are both used when describing visionary experiences in the Bible. In Daniel 2:28, we read of the 'dreams' and 'visions' that came to Nebuchadnezzar and later Daniel describes his own experiences as 'visions that passed through his mind.' A dream that Nebuchadnezzar could not remember came to Daniel in a vision. Sometimes these visions come in the twilight zone between waking and sleeping. This is a time when the enemy can impart projections from the dark realm, and sifting is therefore required, but as our souls heal, there is less 'interference' from this realm. The enemy loves to squeeze through the gaps of your life or any breaches in your soul. In Zimbabwe, if people camped in the bush, they had to check their sleeping bags for snakes if they were not rolled up. The lies of the enemy will slither into our 'sleeping bags' or bodies if we are not vigilant. The enemy comes to steal, rob and destroy (John 10:10). We have to be vigilant to clear our belief systems that the devil has ingrained so deeply in your mind, that they now exert power over certain areas of your life: "The weapons we fight with are not the weapons of the world. On the contrary, they have divine power to demolish strongholds," (2 Corinthians 10:4). Get out of those grooves and create new neural pathways by learning the truth through scripture and speaking it out of your mouth. We take every thought captive to the obedience of Christ. "We tear down arguments and every presumption set up against the knowledge of God; and we take captive every thought to make it obedient to Christ." (2 Corinthians 10:5). I live in a castle town. In the days that this castle was built, any breaches in the walls could have allowed the enemy access. There are a number of 'arrowslits', narrow paneless openings in the castle wall where archers can place their bows, look out across the open country and launch a volley of attack before the enemy gets to the walls. In an unparanoid way, we need to adopt this defensive posture. Check the walls of your soul's habitation daily so that the enemy does not distract you from the deep spiritual work that God is doing, because, as we know, "For our struggle is not against flesh and blood, but against the rulers, against the authorities, against the powers of this dark world and against the spiritual forces of evil in the heavenly realms." (Ephesians 6:12).

Visitations

In my view, there is a distinction between visions and visitations, though some might call visitations 'open visions.' The former are future events to take place whether with eyes open or closed. In the case of a visitation, there are usually witnesses that experience some or all of what's actually happening in real time. Angels appear in dreams and during actual visitations

—the events are physical interactions in the present —the events are actually taking place. The shepherd's in Luke 2, 8–9, saw the angels with their natural eyes: "And there were shepherds living out in the fields nearby, keeping watch over their flocks at night. An angel of the Lord appeared to them, and the glory of the Lord shone around them, and they were terrified." Paul was on the road to Damascus when Jesus appeared in a visitation: "About noon as I came near Damascus, suddenly a bright light from heaven flashed around me," (Acts 22:6). Paul also heard the audible voice of God in this experience. Peter also had a heavenly light experience: "Now behold, an angel of the Lord stood by him, *and a light shone in the prison*; and he struck Peter on the side and raised him up, saying, "Arise quickly!" And his chains fell off his hands. Then the angel said to him, "Gird yourself and tie on your sandals"; and so he did. And he said to him, "Put on your garment and follow me." So he went out and followed him, and did not know that what was done by the angel was real, but thought he was seeing a *vision*. When they were past the first and the second guard posts, they came to the iron gate that leads to the city, *which opened to them of its own accord*," (Acts 12: 7–10). The last part of this verse is reminiscent of an experience I had when I was younger where a door was unlocked, opened and then closed and relocked during a heavenly visitation.

It was 1987. I was working in Tokyo. I lived in an apartment with an Italian woman whom I will call Nina. I was not a Christian at the time, but had recently been exposed to the Bible and was wrestling with the truth of it but was not keen on the church in which I'd heard it read. One night, Nina and I were up late at night chatting. We were having one of those 'meaning of life' conversations. I began speaking to her about the Bible. Soon I found myself preaching about it, which had the effect of solidifying the truth in me and convincing Nina of the veracity of the Gospel at the same time. We ended the conversation with Nina saying that she was going to buy a Bible when she got back to Europe. By this time it was the early hours of the morning. I switched the light off and we settled down to sleep. As soon as I lay back down I began to feel a sense of primal fear. The only thing I can relate this kind of fear to is to an experience I had when I was on safari in Zimbabwe sleeping in a flimsy hut with a grass door. When the camp switched off the generator on the first night, the ground began to shudder as if an earthquake was coming. It was terrifying. A herd of elephant were in the camp sniffing around our hut. At any point they could have trampled us but they didn't. In that apartment in Tokyo, Nina was feeling the fear too. It was like electricity in the body. "Turn the light on," she said. As I reached up to do so, the door, that was locked and latched, unlatched and unlocked itself and swung open. As we watched in abject terror, a vast blue column of light, the colour of blue flame, came into the room and stood before us. The blue light was contained in a geometric shape like a vast pillar stretching to the sky—it was not shadowy or fuzzy at the edges. It was so vast that it rose through the ceiling and up beyond the floors above and beyond. Neither of us said anything, we were so gobsmacked and terror stricken. But we were not in the presence of evil. We were in the presence of good. Of God. And it was awesome. We were awestruck in the truest sense of the word. Just as soon as it appeared, it left. And even though it was capable of moving through walls and ceilings, it relocked and re-latched the door. Nina and I turned to each other and recounted to each other what we had seen. We had seen the same thing. We had both seen the heavenly realm exposed with our physical eyes. The heavens had rended and the manifest presence of God had come to earth in heavenly glory. Even as our hearts opened to receive the truth of the word, the word had manifested before us. Years later when I had fully surrendered my life to Jesus, I was reading about how the angel of the Lord had come to break Peter free from prison. The heavenly light that came unlocked the prison doors, just as the door to that room in Tokyo had been unlocked and our lives had been impacted by heaven coming to earth. In Exodus 24:10 Moses, Aaron, Nadab and Abihu, and the seventy elders of Israel saw the God of Israel come with the colour of sapphire beneath His feet. "and they saw the God of Israel. And there was under His feet as it were a paved work of sapphire stone, and it was like the very heavens in its clarity."

Visions for or from other people

In 2018, I had been a given life shattering health diagnosis. I had to grapple with the very real fear that I might die from ovarian cancer when my three youngest children were barely out of nappies. During this time a man from a church I had once attended called me out of the blue and quoted this: "the serpent that has been sent to kill you will not have its way." That vision gave me life in the form of faith. I had not seen that man for years, nor could he possibly have known about my diagnosis.

Another time, I was preparing for a court case. I knew by the spirit of wisdom exactly what three members of my mother's family were plotting: to take my share of my great uncle's inheritance. One evening I went to a film premiere in London. As the producer of the film (whom I had never met nor spoken to) shook my hand she went into a vision where she saw me as a huge tree that was being stripped of its bark. She saw three people at the base of the tree with old bags of money. She then saw the Lord come between them and the money with a sword. I won the court case with, unusually, full costs. At the time the vision came I needed confirmation from God as to whether to proceed as the trial came at great cost. God is faithful and good.

A friend was in an unhealthy relationship. She came to stay with us for a season during a painful break up. After a while, she reconnected with her ex partner and he planned to come up from the city to the town we were in to begin a process of reconciliation. I began to experience a real feeling of disquiet. When I went into prayer I received a vision regarding my friend's partner. I saw that he had various sealed compartments in his life. God showed me a blonde woman that I described to my friend along with a small child. I shared with my friend that I felt that he had more than one family. My friend did some research. It turned out that my friend's partner did indeed have another family: a blonde woman and a small child. Neither of us would have guessed that this was the case had God not revealed it. My friend went on to commit her whole life to God and have a worldwide deliverance ministry. Dreams and visions can completely transform your life for good and for God!

Another time a pastor's wife whom I had never met was dying in the hospice. The church was praying for her healing. God gave me a vision of a tattoo of a dragon on her arm, and showed me that she needed to break alliance with what that symbol represented. When the pastor went and relayed this there was a surge of life that came into her body.

What are dreams and visions for?

"The heart is deceitful above all things and beyond
cure. Who can understand it?"
Jeremiah 17:9

The purpose of dreams and visions is to direct us and
to help people and even nations through the wisdom
God gives us in dreams. Dreams also help to bring us
to wholeness or integrated healing in Christ, so we
can operate out of our spirits rather than our souls; to
be closer to Him; to converse with Him; to become
more like Him; to bask in His presence. We are invited
to experience Him; to know Him more than biblically.
As we become more like Him, so we become more
effective and powerful and trustworthy as believers.
God has a way of revealing the dark caverns of our
hearts through dreams. Human beings are adept at
hiding their 'dark parts.' To some extent this is
necessary. We can't go round 'spilling the beans' or
our guts all over the place. However, God wants us
healed and whole, so he shows us where our souls
are corrupted by jealousy, hatred, bitterness, greed
and lust for example. These elements of ourselves
may be personified by people appearing as 'types.' A
jealous mistress might be jealousy, a judgemental
priest a punishing aspect of ourselves. A raging bull
might be a personification of our anger. These 'types'
come so that we can repent before God, deal with
these issues and so become more whole.
Psychologists call this 'integration.' These types often
inhabit rooms or settings common to our lives. If you
have a dream like this examine it in the context of
what is happening in your own 'heart' or spirit. If we
don't 'catch a wake up,' in these areas, God may terrify
us with warnings or 'nightmares' to wake us up
before our hearts erode further or we become unwell
as Job 33, 14–18 warns. He tries this way and that
before he slaps you around, metaphorically speaking!

Better that than death. Dreams and visions bring vital and life transforming warnings and directions with them.

Chapter 4. Bible Dreamers

"We both had dreams," they answered, "but there is no one to interpret them." Then Joseph said to them, "Do not interpretations belong to God? Tell me your dreams,"
Genesis 40:8

Old Testament Dreams and Visions

The Jewish people were adept at gaining influence and receiving the mercy and lavish hosting of foreign rulers through the mastering of dream interpretation and via the wisdom of God. This impacted public policy and changed nations. He can do the same today. God used visions in the Old Testament to put His people in places of influence for his purposes as we see in the lives of Moses, Joseph and Daniel. This could happen more often today if only more people took dreams seriously. In the Old and the New Testaments, the word 'dream' appears over a hundred times. There are 21 recorded dreams in the Bible, 10 in Genesis alone. The Hebrews, Babylonians and ancient Egyptians all used dream interpretation. Dreams are the spiritual language of humankind.

"When there is a prophet among you, *I, the Lord, reveal myself to them in visions, I speak to them in dreams.* But this is not true of my servant Moses; he is faithful in all my house. With him I speak face to face, clearly and not in riddles; he sees the form of the Lord.Why then were you not afraid to speak against my servant Moses?"
Numbers 12, 6–8

The extraordinary story of Moses appears in the books of Exodus, Leviticus, Numbers, and Deuteronomy. Moses received visitations from God who appeared as a burning bush and as a cloud on the mountain. He received the ten commandments; and along with Aaron and Miriam, spearheads some of the most extraordinary miracles in the Old Testament as he leads his people out of Egypt in the Exodus. But he did not start out as a likely candidate to lead the Jewish people, though he was God's candidate all along. The life of Moses is an example of how God saves and transforms His people for purpose. The transformational power of God is mind-blowing. Moses had an anger issue. His anger arose from injustice, but his hotheadedness spilled over into murder. He went from being abandoned in a basket (albeit to save his life) to growing up in a king's palace, to becoming a murderer and then on to become the person who led the Israelites out of Egypt! What a life. He is described as someone who 'spoke to God face to face." 'The LORD would speak to Moses face to face, as one speaks to a friend." (Exodus 33:11). Moses had the weighty favour of God upon him. You can have interactions with angels in dreams and in life, but speaking to God, 'face to face,' is also possible. But you might very well have had encounters with angels and or God and not realised it, as God does not always come in a form you might expect. Those messages you may or may not be 'binning' could be direct communications from Him!

In Daniel 4, Nebuchadnezzar has a troubling dream that only Daniel can interpret. The king is depicted as a magnificently powerful tree that gives dominion to birds, beasts and people. The magnificent tree is cut down to earth, and the stump and roots are left to grow wild. The dream, as interpreted by Daniel, represents Nebuchadnezzar's coming downfall: God's judgment on him for his arrogance, but he is warned that if he changes his ways his fate can be avoided. Spoiler alert: He doesn't avoid it. Like the children's book *The Bear Hunt* by Michael Rosen, "he can't go around it, over it or under it, he has to go through it," for "seven times" where Neb basically lost his mind along with his kingdom and was hung out to dry with "the beasts of the field." Best to listen when God warns of coming judgement. Daniel himself had many dreams and visions, mostly related to future kingdoms of the world and the nation of Israel. In Daniel 7, Daniel sees a lion, a bear, a leopard, and another strange, ten-horned beast come out of the sea. The Ancient of Days (God) judges the beasts, and the Son of Man (Jesus) is given dominion over all the earth. The four beasts represent or were symbolic of, human empires to come in later periods of history. Daniel was one who encountered the Ancient of Days (God) in his dreams and visions.

Joseph the dreamer has two dreams that split him from his family (Genesis 37:1–10). In the first dream, Joseph and his brothers are gathering grain into sheaves. Jospeh's sheaf stands upright, but the brothers' bundles of grain bow down to Joseph's sheaf. This winds up Joseph's brothers. Not only is Joseph the favourite son, now he thinks that he's going to rule over the rest of them? The cheek of it! He's the young one and all! Then Joseph has another dream. This time, the sun, moon, and eleven stars bow down to him. This sends his father into a tizzy as well as his brother: "His brothers said to him, "Are you indeed to reign over us? Or are you indeed to rule over us?" (Genesis 37:8 ESV). But justice is served cold when the dream comes to pass. God gives the same message twice but with different symbols to highlight the point. In Egypt, Joseph finds himself in prison due to a false accusation (Genesis 40:9–15). He meets two other prisoners, Pharaoh's former cupbearer and former baker, both of whom had troubling dreams. So troubling that they are emotional. The cupbearer dreams of a grape vine with three branches, which he harvests and presses into Pharaoh's cup. The three branches represent three days between the dream and the cupbearer's restoration to Pharaoh's court. The baker has a dream, too. In the dream, he carries three bread baskets on his head—but the birds eat the bread from them. The three baskets represent another three days —at the end of which Pharaoh beheads the baker, and the birds eat the baker's flesh. I'd have hated to have given that interpretation! (Genesis 40:16–19). Joseph is made Prime Minister of Egypt during the famine— as represented by the sheaves. Egypt is as powerful as the cosmos, as indeed is he, given his extraordinarily high position in Egypt. Metaphorically speaking the power of Egypt and his meteoric position is cosmic: the stars and moon being metaphors or symbols. God's purpose all along was to raise Joseph to second-in-command over Egypt and to save the Egyptians and the Israelites from a horrible famine as predicted by Pharoah's dream in Genesis 41:1–57 ESV: "After two whole years, Pharaoh dreamed that he was standing by the Nile, and behold, there came up out of the Nile seven cows, attractive and plump, and they fed in the reed grass. And behold, seven other cows, ugly and thin, came up out of the Nile after them, and stood by the other cows on the bank of the Nile. And the ugly, thin cows ate up the seven attractive, plump cows. And Pharaoh awoke. And he fell asleep and dreamed a second time. And behold, seven ears of grain, plump and good, were growing on one stalk." Joseph is summoned from prison to interpret this dream, which leads to his rapid promotion in becoming the second most powerful man in the land next to Pharaoh. The brothers have to come begging for grain and bow down to him as symbolised by both sets of dream elements (Genesis 42:6–9).

In the story of Gideon we read of a dream that an enemy, Midianite guard had that was overheard by Gideon arrived just as a man was telling a friend his dream. "I had a dream," he was saying. "A round loaf of barley bread came tumbling into the Midianite camp. It struck the tent with such force that the tent overturned and collapsed."

His friend (turned interpreter) responded, "This can be nothing other than the sword of Gideon son of Joash, the Israelite. God has given the Midianites and the whole camp into his hands." When Gideon heard the dream and its interpretation, he bowed down and worshiped."(Judges 7:13–14). Good thing Gideon used his loaf of bread ('head' in Cockney rhyming slang) took this prediction seriously and defeated the Midianites. Barley bread (symbolic of Gideon) was the poor man's bread, this symbolised the then poverty of Israel as well as Gideon, who were poor, despised, and oppressed. Gideon himself was not mighty and noble, nor strong in and of himself, yet God used him to bring great victory, cheering him on, chapter and verse, through a dream.

Jeremiah, Samuel, Solomon, Amos, Elijah, Ezekiel, Obadiah, Zechariah and Nahum, are among the prophets who took part in a vast prophetic (and poetic) panorama and encountered God through dreams or visions. The exact nature of some of the visionary experiences that people had in the Bible is not always easy to understand. We know they *saw* the word (God) or they *saw* the angel of the Lord or angels. Did Zacharias see the angel Gabriel with his physical eyes or with his internal, spiritual eyes? Did Daniel physically see Gabriel? During 'a vision of the night,' Zechariah spoke with the angel of the Lord in the myrtle trees, as seen in Zechariah 1:10. I believe they did, given my own experience of visitations, that I saw literally with my physical eyes in the present.

What is described by Daniel in chapter 8 of the book of Daniel, encompasses all manner of visionary and auditory states that appear to include trances and possibly translation in the spirit. He saw empires rise and fall on the earth in both the immediate and distant future—one of the visions was 'sealed' for a future time. Daniel was so worn out from his experiences that he described as "beyond his understanding." What all these experiences have in common are unusual ways of *seeing*, of interacting with God beyond what is usually experienced through faith. Faith being the substance of things unseen: "Now faith is confidence in what we hope for and assurance about what we do not (necessarily) see." I added the brackets there. Seeing is believing, but faith is experienced through the living word, Jesus and the word of God—the Bible. These interactions are deeply mysterious and sometimes beyond our human capabilities to fully comprehend them much less describe them, but to encounter God in these ways is irrevocably transformational and awesome in the original sense of the word. I would argue that dreams and visions enlarge faith for the (usually) 'unseen' and for miraculous interventions of all kinds.

New Testament Dreams and Visions

In the absence of speedy modern information services, dreams and visions in the New Testament provided information unavailable elsewhere at a crucial and pivotal time in history, to identify and foretell the coming of Jesus (the promised Messiah) and to establish and rapidly grow His church. As per Joel 2:28, the time of the Holy Spirit coming to inhabit humanity through and post Jesus was being ushered in. The Kingdom of God was to be at hand, literally, to all who believed. In Luke 1:5–23 God used a vision to tell Zacharias, an old priest, that his wife, Elizabeth,

Mary's cousin, would soon give birth to John the Baptist who paved the way prophetically, for his cousin, Jesus. Visions in the New Testament were often directionally life saving. Paul dreamt of a man from Macedonia standing and begging him, "Come over to Macedonia and help us." (Acts 16:9). It would have taken nothing less than a vision from God to convince Ananias, a Christian in Damascus, to visit Paul, the persecutor and murderer of Christians (Acts 9:10). His intelligence alone, in both senses was terrifying and he had a fearsome reputation. But because Ananias was obedient to God's prompting, Paul regained his sight and his eyes were opened to the truth about those he was trying to kill. Where would we be without Paul and the aforementioned Peter's visitations? They were God's instruments to build, establish and spread the church across the Roman Empire to the world. I hope you can see how important, dreams, visions and visitations are.

Chapter 5. Who is Qualified to Interpret Dreams?

"'And in the last days it shall be, God declares, that I will pour out my Spirit on all flesh, and your sons and your daughters shall prophesy, and your young men shall see visions, and your old men shall dream dreams...
Acts 2:17 ESV

Can everyone interpret dreams?

Yes. We all have the ability to interpret dreams, if we will pay the price by learning to do so. Not everyone can initially interpret dreams without help, and those who interpret at a high level like the prophets of the Old Testament, Daniel or Joseph the Dreamer, are reasonably rare, but we all have access to the same Holy Spirit, He can give us all the wisdom we need or He can trust us with. So we all have great potential to grow in this dimension. Daniel was a scholar in the humanities: skilled in the language and, literature of the Chaldeans as well as scripture. I do not think it wise to discount all worldly knowledge. Profound truth is to be found in the study of the humanities, and the wisdom of God is to be seen in all aspects of the world that are good and beneficial, though the ultimate truth of God is revealed through scripture. Look at how mathematics and the sciences reveal the truths of God's order in the universe for example. What is important is that we do not veer off from the truth into the realms of the new age. Paul warns us of this: "Beware lest any man spoil you through philosophy and vain deceit, after the tradition of men, after the rudiments of the world, and not after

Christ." Colossians 2:8. Are there dream interpreters and teachers who interpret at a high level in the courts of kings and statesmen? Yes. Interpreters at this level will have studied the Bible, their own dreams and those of others and been schooled by God for many, many years, and God will have made them with an aptitude for learning and the ability to understand dreams of all kinds: "To these four young men God gave knowledge and understanding of all kinds of literature and learning. And Daniel could understand visions and dreams of all kinds," (Daniel 1:17). But we can all grow in wisdom and character as we apply our minds to learning the language of dreams and put the Bible into practise. Joseph too was highly unusual and highly trained—in both the wisdom of God but also by his life circumstances. Both men were trained to the highest level with the knowledge of the day in very sophisticated circumstances. As was Moses, the prophet, shown by the Bible to have been as close to God as a person can be. These men were great men of character and this is the most important principle of all. "Now Moses was a very humble man, more humble than anyone else on the face of the earth," (Numbers 12:3). God hates a haughty spirit and Jesus was meek. Perhaps this was why Moses qualified to be mentored face to face by God? Both Daniel and Joseph's responses to constantly being threatened with death were resolute. Even when Daniel was chucked in a fire, he would not renounce his God. They did not whinge, complain, or compromise their beliefs. They accepted their fates with Christ like resignation and learnt what they needed to learn in pretty dire circumstances, and in due course they were elevated to lofty positions. God trusted them with high level knowledge thanks to their impeccable characters. The tough times they endured caused them to rely heavily on God and on His supernatural understanding in order to cope with the events of their lives and to acquire the wisdom necessary to interpret and lead their people at a high level.

Though some are highly gifted in this area, in that God has given them a particular 'anointing' or wisdom to interpret dreams, gifting without character will not suffice when it comes to acquiring God's trust. Joel's scripture tells us "And afterward, I will pour out my Spirit on all people. Your sons and daughters will prophesy, your old men will dream dreams, your young men will see visions," (Joel 2:28). God wants to communicate with all of us about our lives and to give us particular wisdom. There are some that can interpret at high level about world events and political and national issues: a Daniel or Joseph anointing if you will, but this is, as far as I am aware, not currently common—neither in the Bible nor in modern life, but we should all be endeavouring to grow in this area as much as possible. As we dedicate time to apply ourselves and grow in this area, so God will sharpen and strengthen us in our in our ability to interpret. Beginner interpreters may need to find someone with skill and understanding to unlock many of the deeper dreams. Job 33:23 KJV says "If there be a messenger with him, an interpreter, one among a thousand, to shew unto man his uprightness:" This verse shows us the gift is reasonably rare. Many think they understand dreams yet they miss the fulness of the interpretation or get a part of it wrong and so the whole dream collapses like a house of cards made by human hands and deception creeps in. A dream has one interpretation. If it is interpreted incorrectly then the truth is unfortunately missed. Happily though God in His mercy often repeats himself, but there comes a time when the warning must be heeded.

Jesus taught his followers to "beware of false prophets, which come to you in sheep's clothing, but inwardly they are ravening wolves." There are false prophets and dream interpreters operating in the world today. We are warned about these people in Zechariah and Jeremiah as well as in the New Testament:, "The idols speak deceitfully, diviners see visions that lie; they tell dreams that are false, they give comfort in vain. Therefore the people wander like sheep oppressed for lack of a shepherd." (Zechariah 10:2). "I have heard what the prophets say who prophesy lies in my name. They say, 'I had a dream! I had a dream!' How long will this continue in the hearts of these lying prophets, who prophesy the delusions of their own minds?" (Jeremiah 23:25–26). "The prophets are prophesying lies in my name. I have not sent them or appointed them or spoken to them. They are prophesying to you false visions, divinations, idolatries and the delusions of their own mind," (Jeremiah 14:14). You do not want to be coming in to agreement with someone who is under the wrong spirit—the doctrine of demons, advertently or inadvertently (2nd realm)—or operating out of 'vain imaginings,' or the soulish realm. "The Spirit clearly says that in later times some will abandon the faith and follow deceiving spirits and things taught by demons." (1 Timothy 4:1). You do not want to be following 'another' or 'the other' to the Holy Spirit. You need to be a mature believer rooted in the word of God; a student of the Bible, led by the Holy Spirit, who quickens the word that you have already studied to your mind as you come to interpret. Believers grow in wisdom and stature. It is not an overnight thing. It is unwise to raise yourself up to lead or teach before time, and an interpreter should have a long record of dreams and visions having come to pass or of interpreting 'correctly,' or 'rightly' as in righteously. Only those in right standing can do this and it takes a lot of skill and training to carry the 'marks of Daniel,' so get started now if you haven't already!

Daniel was taken captive in the Babylonian exile. We know that Daniel was from a noble family, and his nobility extended to his character as well. He was noble in word and deed. He is described as handsome with an aptitude for every kind of learning; he was well-informed and quick to understand complex matters; he was full of wisdom. In today's language, we might say that he was intellectual and sharp witted, very well qualified to teach in the King's palace. Daniel was to train for three years in the language and literature of the Babylonians. He and his Jewish friends were to be assigned rations from the king's table, but Daniel refused to defile himself with the food and asked the chief official who was looking after him for permission to not eat the kings food. From this we understand that he was a man of no compromise, even when faced with death via a despotic and possibly psychopathic king, he and his friends were not prepared to be disobedient to the Hebrew laws. The king's official was wary of getting into trouble but despite his fear of losing his head, literally, God turned his heart to be favourable to Daniel and so he accepted Daniel's request to test them for ten days on vegan food. After ten days, Daniel and his friends looked healthier and better nourished than any of the young men who had eaten the royal food. God was with them! The Bible shows us Daniel had the spirits of wisdom, counsel, understanding and knowledge. The three spirits are aspects of God's character or Godly attributes. The 7 spirits of God are described by John the Revelatory in the book of Revelation 1:4. In Daniel 5:11, we read that his abilities were seen in the culture he lived in and not just by the Hebrew exiles: "There is a man in your kingdom who has the spirit of the holy gods in him. In the time of your father he was found to have insight and intelligence and wisdom like that of the gods. Your father, King Nebuchadnezzar, appointed him chief of the magicians, enchanters, astrologers and diviners." This was an adviser to King Belshazzar, in reference to Daniel's abilities. His humility, skill, faith and diplomacy stood him in good stead in the hostile and often deadly world he was to negotiate. Daniel was a man of great character who put his faith before his own life as we see later in Daniel when he meekly goes to his death in the lion's den as per an edict signed by the King in ignorance. Daniel refused to be paid for his interpretations, as he knew the interpretation was God's. Freely we have received and we give what we have been given for free we should give away for free. Interpretation belongs to God and therefore is not ours to charge for—God freely gives us talents which we can charge for in business or the workplace. Certainly we should never charge to give a dream interpretation or prophecy. This is what clairvoyants, tarot readers and psychics do. For us, it's a 'no no,' it's unbiblical and has the potential to open doors of revelation to other, ungodly sources. As we follow Biblical guidance and guidelines, we can expect God's attributes to grow in us as we focus our attention on Him and his Biblical precepts. God gave Daniel unusual gifts and blessed him, given Daniel always gave God the glory. God caused him to prosper in the gifting of the Lord, due to his obedience and dedication to Him. Daniel kept the faith in an ungodly land despite trials and persecutions. He prayed three times a day in the direction of Jerusalem. He never forgot who he was and who His God was despite all the temptations of the culture around him. He kept himself sanctified in body, mind and spirit as we learn from chapter 1 of the book of Daniel. God placed Daniel in a position of power and influence by allowing him to interpret a foreign ruler's dream. As He does today, God used miracles to identify His messengers or His message. In Daniel 5 we can read the story of the writing on the wall, which is how we get the idiomatic expression 'the writing is on the wall,' meaning, something awful will soon happen, or something will come to an end.

None of the wise men of the land could explain this mysterious and terrifying event, but the queen recommends Daniel to her husband (Nebuchadnezzar's son) as someone able to explain the visitation of the hand and the writing. "In the time of your father he was found to have insight and intelligence and wisdom like that of the gods," (Daniel 5:11)

The rags to riches plot of Joseph's story is worthy of any Hollywood blockbuster. Joseph the Dreamer was clearly a charismatic, talented and handsome man and the favourite of his father, which provoked his brothers to jealousy. Joseph is sold into slavery in Egypt and ends up serving in Potiphar's household where Potiphar's wife tries to seduce him. When he resists out of respect for his boss, she falsely accuses him of trying to seduce her and, as far as we know, he does not defend himself. He ends up in prison, where he behaves impeccably and where, following two episodes of accurate dream interpretation (Genesis 40), his wisdom and gifting come to Pharaoh's attention. What we learn from this is that if we are faithful to God in the trying circumstances of our lives, he will reward us and increase our wisdom. As we model the traits and characteristics of Jesus, so the power of God through the Holy Spirit is magnified in our lives and through our dreams and visions.

Jesus teaches us to 'be holy as He is holy,' 1 Peter 1;16. Moses came to be an exemplary character, but despite his success as a visionary leader, he also had human weaknesses such as a temper, a speech impediment or a terror of speaking, fear and self-doubt. But it was in the desert that Moses' character was refined as it often is with us when we go through 'seasons in the wilderness,' or tough times. These human flaws ultimately contributed to his eventual strengths, given he had to struggle with them and overcome them—this is the process of psychological and spiritual integration whereby some of our greatest weaknesses can become our greatest strengths.

We also see this transformation in the life of Jacob, who in his tenacity wrestled for, and received, God's blessing. However, prior to his personal reformation he was a liar and a deceiver who conned his father for his brother's inheritance before going on the run, during which time, his Uncle Laban gave him a taste of his own medicine by swapping out one wife for another, (Genesis 29:21–30). There is hope for us all, but we must make every effort to have our soul issues healed in order to operate out of integrity. Moses went from having murdered someone to becoming a humble, empathetic and heroic leader. We see this in the way he stood up to Pharaoh and his magicians who must have been terrifying in their displays of black magic. He was patient, self-reflective and full of wisdom. Humility, obedience, having a teachable spirit, and reliance on God and scripture is what caused them to become the great men of God. False humility is not helpful either, and can be arrogance in disguise. We should all be self-reflective and looking to God, the Bible and wise counsellors or friends to keep ourselves in check and in balance: "For by the grace given me I say to every one of you: Do not think of yourself more highly than you ought, but rather think of yourself with sober judgment, in accordance with the faith God has distributed to each of you. "For by the grace given me I say to every one of you: Do not think of yourself more highly than you ought, but rather think of yourself with sober judgment, in accordance with the faith God has distributed to each of you." (Romans 12:3).

In short, we are all 'hard-wired' by God to interpret or understand dreams, but the deeper the character the higher the call, and the vaster the pool of available wisdom—wisdom increases with character. The Bible tells us that Jesus grew in wisdom and stature: "And Jesus grew in wisdom and stature, and in favour with God and man." (Luke 2:52). With the Holy Spirit in us, we too can grow in wisdom and stature in all aspects of our Christian walk including the areas of dreams and visions, as we apply ourselves as diligent students, and followers of both the Bible and the living word: Jesus.

In summary, it takes years of study to reach the Daniel standard, but this does not mean that you cannot interpret your own dreams, you can, and I believe God wants us all to be able to do this with our own dreams but also as we grow in wisdom and discernment to help interpret the dreams of others. Those who carry the 'Daniel code' or interpret at a high level, tend to be scholars or people with an ability to understand academic subjects. But we all have different gifts and abilities and we should help each other so we all grow as one unified body or *ekklesia.* Paul explains this well in Romans 12:4. Skilled interpreters are a gift to the church as much as teachers, pastors or prophets, or any other gifted believer is. It takes a little patience in building up your own, personal *repertoire* or 'dictionary' of symbols, and you need a thorough knowledge of scripture as well as being able to hear the voice of God through the Holy Spirit, but God always rewards diligent students.

Chapter 6. Dream Sources

Are all dreams from God?

"I will praise the LORD, who counsels me; even at night my heart (symbolic of inner thoughts) instructs me."
Psalm 16:7

In my experience, most, but not all dreams are from God, but all are valuable, one way or another. We do not need to dismiss what our own hearts or minds reveal to us regarding our innermost thoughts. This type of reflection is still helpful. In the busyness of life, we do not always have time to meditate on or process what is really going on in the deep recesses of our hearts. Our own souls—hearts, minds and emotions—can give us helpful instruction, though these dreams are not necessarily from God. Arguably, however, God gave us our hearts and minds in the first place, so this is all valid, if carefully and reflectively considered. Carl Jung, the famous psychiatrist, believed that dreams are messages; our minds throwing out information that our conscious minds might have missed. But this too can be seen as a helpful, godly mechanism, with God's creative hand on the lever. The father of psychotherapy, Sigmund Freud, who came up with the therapeutic device of free association, whereby a dreamer interpreted their own dreams to the therapist, in whatever incoherent way they emerged, said, "I must affirm that dreams really have a meaning and that a scientific procedure for interpreting them is possible." Our souls need healing as well as spirits, and soulish dreams can be revealing, or 'telling.' "A dream comes when there are many cares..." Ecclesiastes 5:3. If you are desperate to get married and you dream of a tall handsome stranger, this is likely 'wishful thinking' or your soul driven desires projecting onto your mind. Dreams from our souls can be helpful, we don't need to dismiss them, but they are not necessarily from God.

How do I know if a dream is from God?

"Dear friends, do not believe every spirit, but test the spirits to see whether they are from God, because many false prophets have gone out into the world."
1 John 4:1

As in the case of Nebuchadnezzar and Pilate's wife and the cup bearer and baker, all of whom were emotional over their dreams, if you are gripped or 'troubled' or greatly affected by your dream in some way then it is likely from God and worth pressing in to. Test the spirit of the dream or the interpretation coming through others—is it weighty—does it convict or direct, caution or counsel? If it's from God and you have applied it in context, you should sense 'the penny drop,' a resonance in your spirit. If it takes a while, take heart. At Daniel took hours and weeks over his high level dreams and even needed Gabriel to come and give him an interpretation after battling the Prince of Persia. This indicates that there can be interference from the demonic realm in getting the full interpretation, particularly if the dream is of a corporate nature or non personal. Break through the static and keep tuning in to the third realm for revelation. Don't give up! Wrestle with God for the full interpretation. If God says the same thing twice or even three times, even in different ways, with varying symbolism, or in successive dreams, pay attention. The dream will come to pass. It may well be a warning dream. If the dream rattles you don't assume it's not from God. He may be revealing something dark that you need to know. Is it backed up by scripture coming to mind or do the symbols resonate biblically? If so it's likely from God. As you get closer to Him or grow in character and take care of troubled soul issues, you will have less and less soulish dreams. When you are ready, he will promote you and you will dream less of being in houses with projections of what is going on with you inside them, though those will come if necessary and you will begin to dream of more corporately—of events outside of yourself or your heart issues.

Does the devil or Satan send dreams?

"And no wonder, for Satan himself masquerades as an angel of light."
2 Corinthians 11:14

Satan is not creative, but he is a liar. He appears as an 'angel of light' and can impersonate anyone. Even Jesus, so don't believe everyone who says they have had visitations of Jesus. Examine the fruit of their ministry and see if it backs up their claims. Jesus does however appear in dreams. And I have certainly had this experience. There are lots of reports of Jesus appearing to Muslims in dreams. We have looked at the three realms of influence on a person's life. As is the case with prophesy, we can come under the influence from images projected by satan. As such, we should do everything we can to keep our minds and consciousnesses clean, by being careful of what we watch and read, so that we do not come under the demonic influence of the second realm (the first realm is earth; the second the demonic realm and the third, the realm where God and heavenly beings dwell). "And if your eye causes you to stumble, gouge it out and throw it away. It is better for you to enter life with one eye than to have two eyes and be thrown into the fire of hell." (Matthew 18:9). Here Jesus uses some pretty graphic imagery to encourage us in righteous living.

Jesus was led by the Spirit to be tempted by Satan. We surmise then, that God allowed this. He must have allowed Jesus to see the visions that the enemy showed Jesus in the high places—the kingdoms of this world. Satan moves between the realms, he sees things and he shows people things. He tries to influence us in our minds and through our sourish desires. I have not seen any evidence in my Biblical studies to suggest satan gives dreams and visions but he can influence us through our souls—our mind, will and emotions, through fear, anxiety, stress, guilt and other ungodly emotions. His indirect influence can give us nightmares, or dark dreams. Satan works to deceive us and just as he tries to implant evil thoughts in our minds, he lies to us and tries to influence us as we sleep through our souls. He uses the emotions from our unhealed souls as a springboard for deception, which gets transferred or projected onto the screens of our minds. These emotions can arise from our souls and give rise to emotional turmoil in dreams: nightmares that arise from condemnation rather than conviction—conviction is Godly and encouraging, and arises from spiritual communion with God.

If you see what is happening in the demonic realms it doesn't automatically mean that it originated from the enemy, the gift of discerning spirits is active in sleep as it is in waking life, and God can reveal what is happening in the second realm or the plans of the enemy towards you or others, so that you can pray. Satan cannot use the holy, symbolic language of God that we see in dreams and parables. In the twilight between waking and sleeping he can appear demonically in one form or another and can move between the second and first realms at will. I once 'dreamt' that a demon was crushing my chest. I came to consciousness repeatedly trying to say 'Jesus,' as I came to I was finally able to utter 'Jesus' and the demon left. Was this a dream? No. It was an encounter with a demon sent to terrify me: a demonic attack, I sent it packing. Another time, early in my Christian walk I woke to the sound of a presence walking in my room. I commanded it to leave in the name of Jesus. This experience is like the one described in Job by Eliphaz: Job 4:12–16: "Now a thing was secretly brought to me, and mine ear received a little thereof. In thoughts from the visions of the night, when deep sleep falleth on men, Fear came upon me, and trembling, which made all my bones to shake. Then a spirit passed before my face; the hair of my flesh stood up: It stood still, but I could not discern the form thereof: an image was before mine eyes, there was silence, and I heard a voice, saying..." Satan and his demons make appearances at night when people are vulnerable to attack—between waking and sleeping—between subconscious and conscious states, which was why I needed to come back to full consciousness before I could deal with the demon. Eliphaz may have been having a nightmare— an indirect dream arising from a troubled soul— followed by this demonic attack—a double whammy dirty bomb from the enemy of God and man. We learn that what Eliphaz feared 'came upon him.' Fear was the issue that gave rise to the nightmare that preceded and precipitated the demonic attack. "For the thing I greatly feared has come upon me, and what I dreaded has happened to me," (Job 3:25). Fear gives rise to nightmares. The Bible makes it clear that "our struggle is not against flesh and blood, but against the rulers, against the authorities, against the powers of this dark world and against the spiritual forces of evil in the heavenly realms," (Ephesians 6:12). Satan always attacks us when we are vulnerable, as he did when Jesus was hungry after his extended fast, but the closer we are to God, the stronger our spiritual walls and the harder it is for the enemy to invade. It can and does become impossible for him to infiltrate us as we are transformed from glory to glory and sin dissipates from the landing area of our souls.

> "But if your eyes are unhealthy, your whole body will be full of darkness. If then the light within you is darkness, how great is that darkness!"
> Matthew 6:23

Satan works through 'open doorways,' in a dreamers life to influence a person's spirit as they sleep. If you dream a dark and frightening dream of a back door being left open, God may be trying to highlight to you that there is some unfinished business from the past giving rise to unhelpful emotions, for you to take care of where the enemy (satanic influence) is able to gain access to your life. Jesus warns us to keep our houses (symbolic of our bodies—our spiritual houses) swept clean, we need to get rid of all sin and search our hearts daily to make sure we are doing all we can to keep on the narrow path (a righteous walk). Sin issues are a gateway to the enemy. Satan is a trespasser who looks for 'legal access' to a person's life. The Bible is very clear that unforgiveness gives unclean spirits legal access to attack people. We need to make every effort to close all the doors and windows as we lock up our spiritual houses (bodies) for the night so that enemy intruders cannot 'rob our houses' and sabotage our sleep in the process. The enemy comes to 'steal, rob and destroy'. If our minds are not sanctified by the washing of the word—being transformed by the renewing of our minds—the enemy will transmit evil thoughts and suggestions into our minds as we sleep. A tormenting spirit that a person needs deliverance from can be revealed in a dream so that a person can seek ministry and deliverance. Therefore we need to endeavour to be good soil into which God can use to sow seeds of revelatory knowledge, as per James 1:21: "Therefore, get rid of all moral filth and the evil that is so prevalent and humbly accept the word planted in you, which can save you." We need to make sure that our minds are renewed by the word: "Do not conform to the pattern of this world, but be transformed by the renewing of your mind. Then you will be able to test and approve what God's will is—his good, pleasing and perfect will." Your dreams should always line up with the Bible or reflect the Bible.

Nightmares

Are nightmares from God? God can and does speak through nightmares or 'dark dreams' but you will need to examine the fruit of that dream. Was there a Godly outcome or instruction there? Or was the fruit of the dream terror with no instruction? The enemy condemns, God lovingly convicts. The enemy brings confusion, God brings clarity. Warning dreams can be terrifying but God is trying to wake you up, sometimes literally to pray about something. Nightmares show us where healing is needed or doors need to be closed. Repeated nightmares can reveal an unhealed heart. If you are afraid of being raped or someone breaking into your house, you may well dream of these things until you learn to trust in God as your protector. And not give entrance to fear in your life. Gross, terrifying for the sake of terror or graphically sexual dreams can be the result of guilt and temptation or of satanic provenance, in which case you will need to pray for deliverance. God can still instruct us through these dreams however. Take everything to Him in prayer. Sexual dreams can reveal a longing for deeper intimacy or connection. Take these dreams to God for wisdom or share them with trusted counsellors. Don't discount anything. Note it down. If you are faithful to pray and bring your dreams before God, he will give you the meaning.

Terrifying dreams can and do come from God, as Abram discovered when he gave him a dream of his future descendants, Israel: "Now when the sun was going down, a deep sleep fell upon Abram; and behold, terror and great darkness fell upon him. Then the LORD said to him, "Know for certain that for four hundred years your descendants will be strangers in a country not their own and that they will be enslaved and mistreated there (Gen. 15:12–13). Daniel was terrified by some of his dreams. "I had a dream that made me afraid. As I was lying in bed, the images and visions that passed through my mind terrified me." (Daniel 4:5). Sometimes what feels like a most horrific nightmare will be instructional. I once dreamt that I was taken to a house where these young blonde women tortured me. It was very visceral and unpleasant. But when I woke I understood that what was going on in the dark realm at that time and it's effect on the people of God, as symbolised by me, was emotionally and mentally disturbing. The Bible tells us that "our battle is not against flesh and blood but against the dark powers and the principalities in the heavenly realms." However, this can seem nebulous or abstract at times. It is when we see into the dark realms that we really wake up and take notice and the point is driven home as it were. Don't dismiss nightmares. The inventor of the sewing machine, Elias Howe in a dream in 1845, who had been mulling over the idea of a machine with a needle that would go through cloth. A dream that saw him about to be cooked by cannibals, who were were dancing around a fire in anticipation, waving their spears with glee. He noticed that at the top of each spear was a small hole, with the up-and-down motion of the spears and hole was fixed in his memory when he awoke and is now fixed to your sewing machine. He had that idea all sewn up and patented before you could say Singer! (See what I did there?).

Dark Dreams

As mentioned, during Jesus' trial, Pilate's wife sent an urgent message to the governor encouraging him to free Jesus. God gave a dream to Pilate's wife about Jesus, that greatly troubled her. "Besides, while he was sitting on the judgment seat, his wife sent word to him, "Have nothing to do with that righteous man, for I have suffered much because of him today in a dream." (Matthew 27:19 ESV). Her message was prompted by a dream she had—a nightmare, really—that convinced her that Jesus was innocent and that Pilate should have nothing to do with His case. Abimelech was told by God he was a 'dead man' for taking Sarah into his harem, after essentially being conned by Abraham (Genesis 20, 3–7).
In Genesis 31:24, Laban is warned not to speak to Jacob; in Judges 7:13 As we saw earlier, a Midianite man had the dream of barley bread that turned out to indicate Gideon's victory—this was to be a nightmare for the Midianites! The aforementioned royal baker had his imminent death foretold in a dream; Nebuchadnezzar and Pharaoh all had dark unsettling dreams.

False Dreams

Examine the fruit of the dream. Satan seeks to discourage you. God to encourage you. If you feel discouraged or hopeless about a dream, particularly one that comes just before waking, discard it. In the book of Jeremiah (Jeremiah 29: 4-9). We read of false prophets having false dreams. The purpose being to lead the Israelites into a false sense of security despite their wicked ways. Just as counterfeit prophets can give demonically inspired prophecies, so they can report false dreams: dreams or night visions projected by satan with an ungodly purpose— to lead God's people astray. An incorrect interpretation is a falsity as well.

Does God give Dreams to Everyone, even those who don't believe in Him?

The prophet Joel declared that God would pour out dreams and visions on 'all people' not just on believers: God gives beautiful bouncing babies to murderers and despots as well as good people, we all get to be stunned by the beauty and majesty of his creation: rich and poor alike. As the Bible puts it: He causes his sun to rise on the evil and the good, and sends rain on the righteous and the unrighteous (Matthew 5:45). I often interpret dreams for people who don't know God and this is an opportunity to reveal the dream giver and the dream maker. It's helpful to pray that God will reveal Himself in the process or as you process the dream! I have friends who don't believe in God who come to me with their dreams and I decode them. Do they listen? Yes. Does this bring them closer to God? No hard evidence yet, but I keep interpreting and I keep praying. I have a friend to whom I have interpreted one dream after another, which have come to pass as predicted, but she still won't acknowledge the source. This can be frustrating, but our role as believers is to speak truth and leave the landing of that truth to God.

Chapter 7. Discerning Good from Evil: The Counterfeit

"Not everyone who says to me, 'Lord, Lord,' will enter
the kingdom of heaven, but only the one who does the
will of my Father who is in heaven. Many will say to
me on that day, 'Lord, Lord, did we not prophesy in
your name and in your name drive out demons and in
your name perform many miracles?' Then I will tell
them plainly, 'I never knew you. Away from me, you
evildoers!'"
Matthew 7:21–23

Here is a common analogy for you. If you were to look
at a real or true dollar bill and then a counterfeit bill,
do you think you could tell the difference? They
would look almost the same, but something would be
'off' .'Suss' as my kids would say. It is the same with
teachings that are doctrinally not quite right or
prophecies or visions and dreams given by some
interpreters or teachers that jar or do not ring true.
There is a discordant note to the trained ear.
Sometimes we don't notice that it's off—and it's not
until we analyse what they are actually teaching or
claiming or what the fruit of their ministries or
teachers is, or isn't, that we realise there's something
false slipped in there. One of the significant warning
signs is how they operate personally and how they
present themselves, and how they handle money,
power and platform.

It is not helpful to pay undue attention to the
demonic realm but sometimes we need to deal with it
as Paul did with the girl who had a divining spirit:
"Once when we were going to the place of prayer, we
were met by a female slave who had a spirit by which

she predicted the future. She earned a great deal of money for her owners by fortune-telling," (Acts 16:16). There is a real hunger in these days for understanding dreams and visions and other ways of hearing the voice of God, and this is a good thing. Many are now sitting under the teaching of various dream interpreters and courses. However, there is a mixture in some of the ministries that I have discerned through dreams and visions, and I find this concerning. These are the verses that warn about people who give false dreams for their own gratification or benefit and turn people from God. I believe this happens wittingly and unwittingly. For more on how this functions please study: Jeremiah 14:14; 23:16, 25–27, 32, 27:9–11; Ezekiel 12:24, 13:1,7; Deuteronomy 13:1–5; Zechariah 10:2. If you come into agreement with what a prophet or interpreter is teaching and the revelation comes from the wrong source, you can get sick, go mad and even die (Deuteronomy 13:5). It is instructive to read the whole book of Jeremiah, particularly from chapter 14. I do not want to scare you, but I am advising you to be careful, and really in the first instance, you should be going to God, the revealer of mysteries, and the Bible first. Usually, the fruit of muddy teaching is confusion, which is a sign that something is 'off,' but if you are seduced into agreement with 'ear tickling' teaching in this area you could be coming into agreement with a demonic assignment against you. Know your sources. The only truly pure sources are God and the Bible, because we know in part and prophecy in part. People are not perfect. I'm not, but I have a track record of 24 years of prophecies, dreams and visions coming to pass that I can prove. Make sure any human teachers and interpreters have a track record. You wouldn't go to a brain surgeon who said he was a brain surgeon but had no surgery experience would you? Or one that had done a course but had no experience? It's astonishing how much self promotion goes on in the church, particularly in the Pentecostal/charismatic model. There are problems with other denominations too, all denominations really, so be careful and anchor yourself in prayer and in the word. This is all to say that though the area of dreams and visions is sometimes an adulterated area, we need to be discerning but we also need to trust in God to lead us in faith."Trust in the LORD with all your heart and lean not on your own understanding; in all your ways submit to him, and he will make your paths straight." (Proverbs 3:5–6)

If you don't have the seemingly rare gift of discerning spirits, ask God. All the spirits of God are in the Holy Spirit who is your source along with the Bible! Hallelujah!

The Bible tells us that we will recognise these people by their fruit. In Matthew 7:15 we read this: "Watch out for false prophets. They come to you in sheep's clothing, but inwardly they are ferocious wolves. By their fruit you will recognise them. Do people pick grapes from thorn bushes, or figs from thistles?" Another way of looking at this is what their ministries give rise to—what is the biblical fruit of their ministries—do they model their lives according to the kingdom as illustrated by the lives of the Biblical model we have in Jesus and the disciples and the prophets and teachers? Do Godly signs and wonders follow them? Does healing occur in people's hearts and minds as well as body or does confusion, frustration or double-mindedness result after listening to false prophets and teachers—I find this to be the case and will show you how this operates. Apart from the Bible, the primary tool we have in this potential ball of confusion is the Holy Spirit in us—our internal guide and compass. If after careful prayer and examination of our own humble and righteous hearts (given over to Jesus), we feel uneasy or confused, we should not be listening to certain teachers and prophets. Don't witch-hunt, but err on the side of caution if need be. There are false teachers and prophets active in the church now. These people are among us, and Paul warned us: "I know that after I leave, savage wolves will come in among you and will not spare the flock." (Acts 20:29). They are in churches and in ministries and on platforms near you. Often these people prop each other up with their own platforms, wittingly or unwittingly. I believe some know what they are doing and some are deceived and potentially following the doctrine of demons—operating out of the second realm due to deception, but this is the realm of psychics and mediums, which is why the 'ear tickling' content they peddle is so seductive. Revelation from the second realm, or from their own imaginations, 'vain imagining,' as the Bible calls it in Jeremiah or from the 'doctrines of demons,' can be very compelling as the person will make out they are 'the special one' with the esoteric revelation that you can only get from them, "But we are one body and you have been baptised into Christ not someone else's 'ministry': Is Christ divided? Was Paul crucified for you? Were you baptised in the name of Paul?" (1 Corinthians 1:13). "But false prophets also arose among the people, just as there will be false teachers among you, who will secretly bring in destructive heresies, even denying the Master who bought them, bringing upon themselves swift destruction. And many will follow their *sensuality*, and *because of them the way of truth will be blasphemed. And in their greed they will exploit you with false words*. Their condemnation from long ago is not idle, and their destruction is not asleep." (2 Peter 2:1–3 ESV). Often these people are very attractive or use their sensuality or sexuality or charisma through which the counterfeit operates. People are often 'blinded' by them. But they are not being blinded by the light, as it were.

81

Obviously, when you are learning to interpret dreams you are going to make mistakes. We all do. This is not the same as a prophet in office or authority giving erroneous teaching about dreams and visions or prophecy that you come under, or publicly claiming God gave them a dream and vision that is false—not from God—in order to draw people or money or both to themselves. Learning a new language takes time and practise and acquiring the symbolic language of dreams is no different. It took me years to build up my dream vocabulary and skillset and I'm still learning on a dream by dream basis. Steward your dreams well and God will expand your knowledge and anoint your ability to interpret dreams as you grow in wisdom and stature in this area. But it is very important not to give your dreams to people to interpret unless they have the spiritual track record of interpreting dreams. It could be that they have deceived even the elect: Matthew 24:24 "For false messiahs and false prophets will appear and perform great signs and wonders to deceive, if possible, even the elect." There are prophetic leaders, 'visionaries' and dream interpreters in the church today who are fleecing the flock through their erroneous teachings and some of these flock fleecers are invited by other leaders who somehow don't seem to see who they really are, or are too busy to look into what leaders they invite onto their platforms are up to. Perhaps they cannot discern in the spirit? Or they are blinded by selfish ambition related to their ministries and monetary growth and mutual platform propping and hopping helps all parties. Suffice to say there are false prophets in churches and on platforms, and you may well have come across them. I suggest that you read the book of Jeremiah carefully to fully comprehend this. Proverbs 14:12 tells us, "There is a way that appears to be right, but in the end it leads to death." These false prophets can appear to be right but their words can lead to death, sometimes literally—the wages of sin is death. Don't pay the wages of dodgy ministries, you don't want to come under the dark canopy they sit under.

Discerning the source: God can reveal the counterfeit to you in dreams and visions

"The Spirit clearly says that in later times some will abandon the faith and follow deceiving spirits and things taught by demons." 1 Timothy 4:1

A number of years ago I met a woman who taught dream interpretation at a church I was attending. She was an attractive woman with a very charismatic personality. She had trained under a dreams ministry that was well known at the time. After I had shared an open vision experience, this woman offered to mentor me. She was prominent in the leadership team of our church at that time and I was required to give my prophecies and visions to her so she could check them before passing them on to our pastor. I was fine with this as I was eager to learn. I was later told by the pastor that the woman was passing off my prophecies as hers. At the time, I had only been a believer for about 5/6 years but the Lord had been training me on how the spiritual realms operate at my previous church: through my actual experiences of dreams and visions lining up with biblical teaching. This is how I have learnt to discern the counterfeit. This spirit of discernment has sharpened me in my dream interpretation training as well. During one teaching session, when she led us into visionary experiences, where we were required to see angels, other people would see what she asked them to see but I would not. Only God can create visions or 'encounters' as they are often called. Anything else is dreamt up by the person leading the encounter. Jesus is not a genie to be summoned, or a person who has dates and times fixed into a diary for Him by a secretary. It is always wise to think things through theologically before 'going along' with something *even if that person has been given a platform.* Since I did not see what she was asking us to see, I presumed I was wrong. God gave me a vision. I saw the woman in a fast red sports car. She was wearing black sunglasses and a scarf ensemble like a 60s movie star. It was disturbing as I knew what the vision meant straight away. The vision elements signified she was in a dangerous worldly vehicle and the dark sunglasses revealed that her sources were dark. Like a film star smiling at the paparazzi before she took off in the car on roads that looked like the ones that Grace Kelly drove on (Grace Kelly died after coming off a similar road). Red might not always signify danger or anger, a colour that can signify, life and passion and many other things within context, but it did in this case. I ignored some of the warning signs as I really liked this woman; we became friends and she began inviting me to her house and into her confidence. It soon became clear to me that she was attracted to a married man on the leadership team. She had been telling me her new theology that was 'off.' This doctrine (of demons) was a teaching that would allow her to be closer to the man she wanted and to minister with him alone. When she explained it, it seemed to make sense but as soon as I left her house I became confused—our God is not a God of confusion. Back home, after speaking to my rational husband, I came back into my 'right mind.' There is a real danger of coming under the counterfeit prophetic, and there is more to this story. Confusion itself, comes from the dark realm—where watcher spirits dwell and communicate counterfeit messages onto the earth and into the minds of people— including the unhealed, unsanctified or otherwise corrupted minds of believers. When I was in her house I came 'under' the source of her information—

the second realm/doctrine of demons—but as soon as I left her house I came back into my 'right' or 'righteous' mind. During this time of questioning, God gave me the following dream:

I was in a hotel lobby. The carpet of the lobby was patterned orange and black—dangerous colours in the context of this dream. Jesus walked towards me with some of His followers and embraced me, but he looked disappointed despite the love in his eyes. I knew then that He did not want me to follow this woman but to turn back and follow Him. I had looked to her to be my mentor, when He alone should have been the one to teach me through the Holy Spirit.

Did this woman know she was operating from deceiving spirits? Was she sincerely deceived or deceiving sincerely? I don't know if she was a witting or unwitting victim of the enemy, but our battle is not against flesh and blood but against the dark pores and principalities that are bent on destroying us. We love the person, and I did, but we must be careful not to 'come under' a dark canopy as we can be led into bondage this way. I think of the witness of the Holy Spirit like a sonar echo. Or the sound of a child's heartbeat beating within us. If we are one with the Holy Spirit as a child in utero is one with a woman through sharing the same blood system, it is harder for us to become deceived. Sometimes people are operating out of a mix. Should you give them the benefit of the doubt? Doubt is never beneficial but God can correct us if we are wrong.

You cannot serve God and mammon: ""No one can serve two masters. Either you will hate the one and love the other, or you will be devoted to the one and despise the other. You cannot serve both God and money." (Matthew 6:24). If money is the main draw, it usually comes with a manipulative spirit of coercion and a marketing of 'esoteric' knowledge, as well as fostering a dependency on the ministry rather than on God—this will be where a 'mix' can come in. A ministry or person may consider their motives pure and think that they should be supported financially in their gifting, but they have become adulterated—the pure flow of the Holy Spirit becomes muddy. Money can be so easily corrupting. Go to the pure source, "My people have committed two sins: They have forsaken me, the spring of living water, and have dug their own cisterns, broken cisterns that cannot hold water," (Jeremiah 2:13). Look at the way people operate and see how it lines up with the Bible. Once you have searched the scriptures and find no precedent for the way they are operating, don't take the risk. Come out and be separate; 'touch no unclean thing' unless you too should become infected. You do not want to get into bondage, or worse. 2 Corinthians 6:14 says "For what do righteousness and wickedness have in common? Or what fellowship can light have with darkness?" God can correct us if we are wrong and He can also correct them. We can trust Him to deal with all of us. Incorrect interpretation can have serious consequences for both parties as you do not want to come into agreement with the wrong spirit— ie. a demonic spirit that can then have access to your life. Nor do you want to sit under a dark canopy, lest you become darkened in your understanding.

Why does this happen?

There could be a lack of accountability. A person or a ministry might have started off well, and the person might be very gifted—there are lots of gifted clairvoyants and psychics for example, but they are getting their revelation from the second heaven— watcher spirits or demons that are simply popping the relevant information and often in detail, into their heads—but it is character and how people conduct themselves behind the scenes as well as in front of the cameras that matters especially in financial matters and how they treat people working for them. Are they sincerely wrong or wrong sincerely, ie. Are they aware of what they are doing or not? I think both scenarios are operating in the church. There is a lot of exposure of it happening lately and I expect it to continue. Perhaps, as their ministries have developed, satan has managed to infiltrate the walls of the ministry or person through human weaknesses or sin. Lots of ministers and teachers are enticed by money, power, platform and sex—there are organisations that are infected 'across the board' in this area; an entire church culture can be infected by a corrupt leadership. We can be very good at deceiving ourselves or inventing or changing doctrine when we want something of the flesh or want to excuse a behaviour that is not of God. Deception can be very subtle and we are warned starkly that even the elect will be deceived. Money in particular can be blinding and it can be all too tempting to want to monetise a gifting that should be freely given. Daniel and Joseph are role models as regards prophetic leadership. Often these ministries use 'smoke and mirrors' to make out they know more than they do, as they have volumes of content to peddle, and perhaps feel under pressure to 'produce.' One way or another, they will have given way to the counterfeit or second heaven, and thus, wittingly or unwittingly (via a mix of what seems Biblical with a dash or two of counterfeit or dodgy theology thrown in), they are following the doctrine of demons. There will be a mixture—of clay (flesh) and iron (Godly teaching or principles). The Bible is clear on these matters and if what they are doing does not line up with the plumbline of the word don't listen to them, much less come under their teaching or authority. If ministers have made a business out of their gifting, that business will be like a lion that needs feeding with meat or something that looks like meat. Sometimes this 'meat' will be 'ear tickling stuff,' and the theology will be a degree or two off but with potentially catastrophic consequences. Remember that counterfeit dollar bill? It looked like the real deal, it may have even acted like the real deal—as in being exchanged as legal tender. But on very close inspection you will find that there are details on that bill that are not accurate. Believers need to be rigorous with the truth and themselves so they do not become involved with an unholy transaction process.

Chapter 8. Dream Types

"For God may speak in one way, or in another, yet man does not perceive it. In a dream, in a vision of the night, when deep sleep falls upon men, while slumbering on their beds, then He opens the ears of men, and seals their instruction. In order to turn man from his deed, and conceal pride from man, He keeps back his soul from the Pit, and his life from perishing by the sword."
Job 33:14–18

Dream or Night Vision?

"He had a dream in which he saw a stairway resting on the earth, with its top reaching to heaven, and the angels of God were ascending and descending on it."

The story of Jacob's ladder is a well-known biblical narrative found in Genesis 28:12. Jacob, fleeing from his brother Esau's anger after deceiving their father to obtain the blessing meant for Esau, sets out on a journey to his uncle Laban's house. As night falls, Jacob has an extraordinary vision regarding the future of his descendants that became the nation of Israel. "And he came to a certain place and stayed there that night, because the sun had set. Taking one of the stones of the place, he put it under his head and lay down in that place to sleep. And he dreamed, and behold, there was a ladder set up on the earth, and the top of it reached to heaven. And behold, the angels of God were ascending and descending on it! And behold, the Lord stood above it and said, "I am the Lord, the God of Abraham your father and the God of Isaac. The land on which you lie I will give to you and to your offspring. Your offspring shall be like the

89

dust of the earth, and you shall spread abroad to the west and to the east and to the north and to the south, and in you and your offspring shall all the families of the earth be blessed." (Genesis 28:10–17 ESV)

Night Visions and Literal Dreams

Literal Dreams/Night Visions usually play out like a movie. You do not need to decode them. You watch the movie God plays for you and you know it's going to happen.

As I slept I had a vision of a teenaged boy I knew sitting in a park wearing his school uniform with a group of other children also in their school uniform. This young man was going through a very difficult period in his life, with lots of disruption and difficulties in his home. I saw the young man in a park under trees taking drugs with his friends from a paper wrapper. I later discovered that this was the actual park that groups of children went to to take drugs. The application of this dream was that I was able to bring the person the help they needed and to stop the dealing of drugs at the secondary school.

Example of a literal dream or vision that came to pass:

As I lay sleeping I saw a large stone oblong building that looked like an English church, without a steeple or adornment of any kind. I saw people coming into the downstairs area of the church through the side of the building. I then saw other buildings, some looked like old Welsh Chapels. As I came out of this night vision— for that is what it turned out to be, as in, it was something I was seeing for the future that was the actual place—I heard a voice tell me, "And this house will be a house of refuge." When I woke up I knew that my husband and myself, who were planning on a move to Wales, the country of Revivals, should indeed be moving to Wales. Further, we clearly should buy buildings in Wales! Thereafter we followed a wild goose chase to various parts of Wales where my husband and myself tried to buy defunct Welsh Chapels that were going to be turned into funky homes rather than places of worship. We repeatedly failed in this pursuit, but a year later, a house came up for sale, we tried to buy it but God gave us a very specific figure that we should offer. They did not take the offer, so we stood our ground and went off and rented for the best part of a year. Some time later, we began looking for a house again. When we began praying, my 6 year old son had a vision of the two stone lions outside the property that I had previously I dreamt about. We looked online and saw that the house we had previously made an offer on was now up for sale again. We made our top offer just before the property went to auction. We bought the property for 30K less than we offered approximately a year before. The house is the stone oblong building I saw in the dream (though it was covered in render when we bought it) and it is indeed being used as a house of refuge in many ways.

A demonic visitation

I'd woken up screaming. My mother was now with me in the lounge of our house in Africa. I was still jumping and screaming, even though I was fully awake. I was 5 or 6. The baby snakes that were jumping up my legs were still there. I could see them with my natural eyes. They were like baby black mambas, but they had yellow markings. I had been seeing these snakes when I was asleep, but I could see them awake too. I had been having a night vision and in my waking state, the vision was there, before me, and I could see it with my natural eyes. I was leaping about as if my legs were on fire.

In those days, I was not a believer in Jesus, and neither was my mother. At the time I had the dream, my mother was practising astrology, numerology (not biblical numerology; God is a master numerologist and the earth and the universe and all life is mathematically ordered; I speak of demonic numerology) and palm reading. The Bible makes it clear that the only acceptable method of foretelling is through the Bible or communications from God through the gifts of the Holy Spirit. True prophets get their dreams and visions from God. At the time I lived in Africa where witchcraft and its manifestations are very real and widespread. My father, who my mother had recently left, had taken me to see a witch when I was two, to help with an allergy I was suffering from. I had connections to the dark side (second realm) through these links and I was already a traumatised child based on the fracturing of my family which left a gateway open for the enemy, but also via the sexual abuse I was receiving from an uncle who was a follower of a guru from an eastern religion. There is the earthly realm in which we operate, but the heavenly realms are right here with us, as Jesus said, "The Kingdom of God is at hand," (Matthew3:2). We could reach out and touch them if God were to open them up like He did for Jacob with His ladder: we could, and can see them. They are not 'up there' as it were. Even though we can't ordinarily see these realms, we are nevertheless influenced by them for good or ill, and it is very much in our interest to discern, through the Holy Spirit in us which is which or which is witch! In my childhood experience with the snakes, I believe satan was trying to frighten me, or lay claim to me, or at the very least, to influence me through this projection or manifestation of snakes. And it was working, I was terrified. I can't quite remember the outcome. My mother must have calmed me and sent me back to bed. This was my first recollection of seeing the spiritual realm with my naked eyes, but it wasn't to be the last. Though the enemy can produce signs and wonders, only God can create life or bring about miracles of nature such as with the parting of the Red Sea or the flood. Pharaoh's sorcerers 'counterfeited' three miracles of Moses and Aaron—the staffs turning into snakes, blood in water, and the production of frogs—to convince Pharaoh that the God of the Hebrews was no more powerful than the gods of Egypt (Exodus 7:10–12, 7:14–22; and 8:1–7). However, their enchantments could only counterfeit the power of God. Aaron's rod was superior and 'swallowed up' their inferior displays of the paranormal. "This is the finger of God" (Exodus 8:19).

As a reminder, there are generally two ways of seeing spiritually. Internal and external visions, but this was a demonic visitation. An internal vision of God is seen with the imagination, or in the 'mind's eye.' These visions or visual pictures that come into the mind, usually do so unbidden or when in an attitude of prayer before God, they are not 'summoned up,' or 'worked up.' Of course you could dismiss them as figments of the imagination. The point is, what is the source of them, and do they carry meaning beyond the obvious physical interpretation? God communicates through internal and external visions, and through visitations just as he communicates to us through the visual language of dreams or through answers to prayer—which of course one could dismiss as coincidences, but I believe more often than not, these are 'God incidences.' If you are unsure, ask yourself the question. Does this seem good? Or pure or lovely? Then it is likely God. If not, then the image you see may be generated from yourself—as in your own soul or imagination—or by the enemy of your spirit—satan. Be alert, the enemy can turn up in a visitation too. Satan projects images onto the mirror of our souls that then find reflection in our minds, that we then project in turn. This is how evil proliferates. The more damaged our souls are the more reflections satan projects and we project in turn. God communicates spirit to spirit, as he does so through dreams. This is so powerful, given the mind will and emotions (soul) are not interfering with what God is trying to say to us. God is true to his divine, creative nature, he does not 'copy' or project, he instigates and creates. He does not force his conversation or advice upon us, rather he invites us into divine relationship and divine conversation. It is up to us to respond or not, and the more we respond, the more information we will get, often life changing or life altering in the best possible way. You may even dream of angels. You will certainly have a conversation of one kind or another with God.

Lucid Dreaming

Lucid dreams are when you know that you're dreaming while you're asleep. You're aware that the events flashing through your brain aren't really happening. But the dream feels vivid and real. You may even be able to control how the action unfolds, as if you're directing a movie in your sleep. Lucid dreams are most common during rapid eye movement (REM) sleep, a period of very deep sleep marked by eye motion, faster breathing, and more brain activity. You usually enter REM sleep about 90 minutes after falling asleep. It lasts about 10 minutes. As you sleep, each REM period is longer than the one before, finally lasting up to an hour. During dreams, our eyes and brains respond similarly to how they react to images when we're awake. We are watching the vision on the screens of our minds. God appeared to Abimelech, king of Gerar, in a nighttime dream. God stated flatly that Abimelech 'is a dead man' for taking Sarah as his wife, since she is a married woman (Genesis 20:3; 20:17). When Abimelech protests that he did not know this, God agrees that Abimelech acted with integrity and had not yet touched Sarah, albeit because of God's own intervention (Genesis 20:6). God gives Abimelech a choice about whether he will live or not. He is to return Sarah to Abraham. When he does so, Abraham will pray, and Abimelech and his household will live. Otherwise, they will all die. Apparently, this is the end of God's conversation with Abimelech. When morning comes, Abimelech will quickly act on what the Lord has said to him. Lucid means 'completely intelligible' or 'easily understood.' Given this was the case in the above example, I believe that lucid dreams can occur today and God can interact this way with people.

Angels

In Matthew 1:18–21 Joseph discovers that his intended bride, Mary, the mother of Jesus, is pregnant by the Holy Spirit. Given Mary was pregnant before marriage, she would have been disgraced and possibly stoned were her condition to be discovered. As such, Joseph "had it in mind to divorce her quietly so that she would not be disgraced." God makes his position to Joseph absolutely clear, by sending him an angel in a dream, thereby assuring him that it was good for him to marry Mary. In the Bible, angels terrify people into submission and then instruct you not to be afraid! As in the case of the nativity shepherds. which is why they usually hilariously tell people quivering with fear 'not to be afraid!' Ultimately, this must have been such a reassuring and comforting experience for him. God wasn't taking any chances with whether Joseph was going to hear him correctly or not by speaking to him in 'a still small voice for example.' The angel then goes on to quote the prophet Isaiah who prophesied the circumstances of the birth, life and death of Jesus. Jesus will become the saviour of the world: "because he will save his people from their sins." To his credit, and as a testament to his lack of stupidity, Joseph did exactly as the angel commanded—it's always best to take direction or correction via an angel as a command! The three astronomers or wise men who came to visit the baby Jesus in Jerusalem were warned by an angel not to return to their own country by a particular route to avoid Herod who was cunningly fishing for information about Jesus so he could kill him. Wise men indeed, they took another route home. Mary and Joseph were again visited by an angel in a dream who warned them to escape the clutches of the megalomaniacal King Herod by fleeing to Egypt. This also fulfilled the old testament prophecy "out of Egypt I called my son." (Hosea 11:1). Finally, after Herod's death, an angel of the Lord appeared to Joseph in a dream and told him he could return to the land of Israel, but when he returned to Israel, and in answer to his concerns about the bloodthirsty Archelaus being in power, he had another dream in which he was warned to go to Galilee. Some of these Biblical kings make Bluebeard look good. We know that angels are "ministering spirits sent to help us" and they do, whether we are aware of this or not. Who knows what is happening in deep sleep? But God can 'bring all things to remembrance.' "But the Advocate, the Holy Spirit, whom the Father will send in my name, will teach you all things and will remind you of everything I have said to you." (John 14:26). Ask God to help you to remember angels in your dreams and to point them out to you.

The angel was about nine feet tall, but perfectly proportioned. He had dark blonde, wavy hair and was

*wearing a long white tunic, with a simple rope sash
around his waist. He had massive wings that rose up
above his shoulders and tipped down by his calves. He
was standing with me and Jill. We were both about 8.
Jill and I were holding hands. The angel gently took my
hand from Jill's. The next day at school, Jill walked up
to me with her arm around Sarah. "I have a new best
friend now," she said. I was taken aback, but not too
upset, given, if I was honest with myself, she really
wasn't the right kind of friend for me, and neither was
Sarah, as it turned out, who I had also been friendly
with. They did not bring out the best in me, rather they
appealed to my baser nature.* Is God interested in
speaking to children and directing them? I believe he
cares very much about the lives of his children,
whatever their ages, and intervenes in their lives
where necessary. Here is an example of a foretelling
dream with an angel sent to help me. The Lord was
showing me that my friendship with Jill was going to
end. He prepared me for it, so when the time came, it
was less of a shock to my natural self because the
Lord had already prepared my spirit for the event to
come. In His kindness, He comforted me in advance,
as well as prepared me. You could even say that he
healed my soul in advance through the dream as I do
not recall sorrowing over this experience and my
friends were and have always been as family to me,
given my relationships with my family of origin were
painful.

Angels are mentioned 365 times in the Bible. You
encounter them in waking life and in dreams, as Jacob
did: "Jacob also went on his way, and the angels of
God met him. When Jacob saw them, he said, "This is
the camp of God!" So he named that place Mahanaim,"
(Genesis 32, 1–2). He later wrestled with God in one
of the most baffling and extraordinary events in the
Bible (Genesis 32, 24–31). Angels appear as men in

my experience, as well as with wings as in my dream with Jill (Hebrews 13:2).

I was walking in Hyde Park in London. Suddenly a team of gardeners were there. I noticed a very tall, black man with unusual features. He was wearing a large cross. For some reason I knew I needed to talk to him. I went over and introduced myself and he walked along one of the paths with me. We chatted about our Christian experience—I had not been a believer in Jesus for long. When we'd finished chatting I asked him if he had any advice to me. "Stay on the narrow path," he said. By this he was referring to the biblical warning: *"Enter by the narrow gate; for wide is the gate and broad is the way that leads to destruction, and many are those who enter in by it."* What he was saying was stay close to Jesus, who is described in the bible as being The Way—the only way to God, truth and eternal life. The broad way, is the way that most people are bound and it is not a good ending and will ultimately lead to destruction. It was a salutary warning, and one that comes back to my mind repeatedly when life's temptations come. I walked on for a moment, but then thought of something else I wanted to ask my gardener friend, whose given name was John. *I returned to where the team of gardeners had been. They weren't there. I asked another member of park staff where they were. He was baffled. There was no team of gardeners in that part of the park that day.* Like Jacob, who wrestled with God, I challenge you to wrestle with God for more dreams and for the meaning of them, so that you can be a conduit of this extraordinary gift. It will impact you and the world around you in extraordinary ways.

Translation & healing in the spirit with the audible voice of God

One night as I slept I saw this: *I was going up a hill in the cool of the evening. An Orthodox Jewish man and his daughter were coming down the hill. The daughter, about nine or ten, was limping. As I drew near to them I said to the man that I knew it wasn't really appropriate for me as a woman, and a Gentile one at that, to ask to do this, but I explained that I was a follower of Jesus and that I believed He (Jesus) wanted to heal his daughter. He agreed to let me lay hands on her knee and pray. As I ministered healing in the name of Jesus, I felt the bones move under my hands. I want to be clear about this. I felt this physically, under my hands. I believe I was translated in the spirit and the healing took place.* As I woke up I heard the audible voice of God quoting scripture to me. "Healing is the children's bread."
All my senses were alive in a natural way during this experience, as they would be in a natural landscape.

As above, in the 2000s I had a series of vivid dreams where I was in Israel. *As I was coming out of each dream into the twilight of waking from sleep—that strange suspension between two worlds, I heard the audible voice of God quoting scripture to me. In the one dream, I was telling an Israeli taxi driver about Jesus.* As I woke God was quoting this scripture to me: "For Christ himself has brought peace to us. He united Jews and Gentiles into one people when, in his own body on the cross, he broke down the wall of hostility that separated us." Ephesians 4:13

Chapter 9. All the Wonderful Things That God Can Do!

Remember the Doctor Seuss book *Mr Brown Can Moo?* It has the phrases:

Oh the wonderful things that Mr Brown can do. He can go like a cow, he can go moo! Moo! Mr Brown can do it. How about you? He can go like a bee, Mr Brown can buzz. How about you? Can you go buzz buzz. He can go like a cork, pop, pop, pop! Mr Brown is smart, as smart as they come, he can do a hippopotamus chewing gum. Grum grum, grum grum, grum grum grum! Boom boom boom, Mr Brown is a wonder, boom boom boom Mr Brown makes thunder. He makes lightening, splat, splat.

This was a favourite childhood book and a favourite of my children's too. How about you? (Sorry). The point I am going to make is that God can do all manner of things. He is such a wonder he invented thunder, and lightning—and enlightening through dreams. He is infinitely creative, the best author of all and the progenitor of your dreams. Even some of those you ignored. Shame on you! Just kidding. Remember the child like wonder of books? Of engaging with stories that caused you to travel in your mind? The greatest author of all is ready to write and dream with you. He is wanting to engage with his innately creative child—you—whether you think you're creative or not. You are, everyone is, though this deep well of imagination where creativity also resides is often 'untapped' in many people. I still get a thrill when I read a Dr Seuss, Roald Dahl or a Spike Milligan book. God is full of humour and wonder. The Bible tells us that he sits on his throne and laughs! Let's engage the wonder, through dreams and visions. What have you got to lose that you haven't already lost? What have you got to gain, again, and a-gain, and a-gain? An infinite gain! Let's look at all the wonderful things that God can do through dreams:

God can comfort and reassure in dreams:

Though the physical landscape of my childhood was stunning, and the world of my imagination was one I escaped to daily, my internal landscape was often terrifying and confusing as I never felt safe. I grew up during a war and my parents had been warring before they divorced and then I was at war with a sometimes violent step parent, all of which gave rise to much fear and anxiety that the enemy seized upon as illustrated earlier. God knew this and was with me. He also gifted me with the ability to laugh. A lot. Humour and comedy were some of my richest companions as a child, along with books and art, and they still are. When times were tough, God was there for me—through my wonderful grandparents who were like surrogate parents, wise teachers and through friends. My brother was a dear companion. There was joy and pain, and lots of obstacles to overcome. Sometimes I felt trapped, and fear would give rise to nightmares. One night I was dreaming that I was being chased through a dark forest. My home life at the time was very difficult. I grew up in a neglectful and abusive environment, and I did not feel that I had anywhere to run or to hide. But in the dream, an angel appeared and I stopped running. The angel appeared to reassure me that I was going to get through the dark forest and that God was with me. This angel managed the situation and gave me strength, as in the case of the angel and Jill. You could ask me why God did not rescue me from the abuse that I suffered. This is a sensible question, and I do not have all the answers, but this is not the place for a thesis on suffering or the nature of good and evil. There are other books that explain this well. However, I do know that God sent people into my life to help me and to sustain me, I had wonderful maternal grandparents, but I still went through suffering. To live is to suffer, it is part of life, but God gives us the strength to get through life, and he wants to give us the tools we need to cope. And yes, he does rescue us. I have been rescued from death in a number of ways, but perhaps those are stories for another book.

God can correct and encourage in Dreams and Visions

When I was in the process of writing this book, I did a lot of research. Believers are works in progress and only see in part or the parts that God sees fit to impart. We do not all have the answers. Some of this research, by well known teachers of dreams and visions conflicts. Sometimes I wrestled with some of the information I was reading and sometimes I was in agreement, but it was all causing me to digress from the original mandate of this book, which was to write from my own experience. During this time I had the following dream:

I was at someone's dinner party that I did not recognise. I had brought some roast beef. I left the beef and then went off to do something else. When I came back I looked for the beef. It was in an old oven—small and white, like a vintage oven from the 60s or 70s, there was an orange flower pattern on the oven door that was broken and falling off and propped up by pans. The meat was now overcooked at the edges. A woman came into the kitchen with a chemical solution that she was mixing to dye someones hair. As I stood

*with the beef. Some of the solution splashed on the
corner of the beef. I had to cut that bit off.*

The dream showed me that I should preside over my
own 'meat': meat signifies maturity and character in
the bible. I should not 'overcook it' nor try to make it
more 'palatable' and I should get it out in good time.
There have been a number of prophecies about this
book and its timing. The meat also signified the
maturity I have gained and have to offer corporately
—as signified by the dinner party, having been a
dreamer all my life and my two and a half decades of
study in this area, not counting the many years of
study of other subjects that God has used in my
interpretation training. Really, I have been in training
since the 70s, the age of the oven, from when I was a
small child receiving dreams and visions. Also the
oven was of vintage style—which is my style and I
don't refer to my age here, though that is pertinent
too! Prophets, or if you prefer, mystics, or visionaries,
are born, not made. The hairdresser, was there as I
was tempted to 'dress up' or change my views
because of other people's revelation: something
chemical or artificial. I was doubting the meat I had
received directly from source. I felt conflicted about
exposing myself to public scrutiny by taking the meat
out of the oven, as it were, through this work. *What if
I am wrong? Others appear to be wrong in some areas?
What if I am deceived over some of the content of this
book?* The chemical 'solution' was a grey/blue/white
mix that fell on the corner of the meat and
adulterated it, which symbolises man's thinking
rather than God's. Blue and white are often colours of
heaven and purity, but this was a mix of thinking or
'stinking thinking' that I needed to correct. The 'grey
areas'—reveal overthinking, given grey matter refers
to the brain—leading to a mix of black and white. The
meat was now overcooked on the edges, which
symbolised the danger of 'overcooking of the

revelation.' I understood that I needed to be brave and offer the meat that I have and be 'sincerely wrong' rather than 'wrong sincerely' if need be. The old 70s oven also showed me that I must not go back to old feelings of inadequacy or 'being wrong' or 'shamed' as I had experienced in my family of origin. This experience points up how the enemy tries to persuade us to keep quiet when we have information that might help people.

God can tell you about major events that are going to happen

There are lots of warning dreams in the Bible, usually involving angels. My daughter often gets warning dreams, some are of national importance. Our family was recently trying to buy a building to be used to benefit and impact community through the arts. There was much opposition to our acquiring this building, particularly from an angry neighbour who wanted the building and was already squatting part of the land attached to it. We were having our very own Joshua season of events! During the build up to waiting to discover whether we were to be successful in our bid, my daughter had the following dream that I quote from her dream journal:

"I dreamed I was in the courtyard and the building door was open. I looked inside and Ralph[7] (our neighbour) was in there with a BBC Reporter and a film crew. I started shouting and told him to get out. Fast forward and I'm on the roof of the building and down below me is the French President Macron. I accidentally slip off the roof and fall on top of Macron.

---

[7] not his real name

He was very annoyed with me and he scowled and went bright red in the face."

This dream sounds bonkers, but when you discover as we did, that we heard the building was officially ours the day we saw on the BBC that Macron had been re elected, it makes sense! Soon afterwards there was a public event where our neighbour was arrested—a big red faced public scene like the one in the dream had taken place. Our neighbour is French, thus the symbol of Macron. In the dream, my daughter is on a high place (roof/Godly position) receiving the revelation, and 'sliding it down from heaven to earth,' coming in to land right on top of the day Macron gets elected. The neighbour in question also has a French surname. The roof is the covering, God's covering for us for events to come, and the fact that He 'had it covered.' God has a sense of humour too and loves puns and wordplay. It's great living under His roof!

God can correct in dreams

"The heart is deceitful above all things, And desperately wicked; Who can know it? I, the LORD, search the heart, I test the mind, Even to give every man according to his ways, According to the fruit of his doings." (Jeremiah 17, 9–10).

Most of our dreams are to do with our own lives. We all need to be open minded and not dismiss where and how we need correction. God often speaks about the condition of our own hearts through dreams. God uses dreams to reveal aspects of our own dark hearts so that we can be healed and become more successful in our lives. Heart dreams can be easy to dismiss as we may not 'like them,' or recognise unattractive aspects of ourselves—often personified by other people or animals or other elements. A raging bull might appear to show you that you are easily 'triggered' into losing it. If you are apt to open your mouth and speak without thinking, God might show you a mouthy person to illustrate this character trait that needs dealing with. God wants us healed and whole with all our characteristics redeemed and in the light as they were created to be. Over the course of my Christian walk, God has given me dreams where he has shown me where 'the narrow path lies.' Before I was a believer, I hung out on the wide path and spent the first decade or two of my adult life doing what I pleased more than what might please God. I have to watch this prior conditioning not 'sneaking up on me.' I have to be zealous in guarding my path so that I do not 'backslide' into areas of previous conditioning. As Jesus puts it: "Enter through the narrow gate. For wide is the gate and broad is the road that leads to destruction, and many enter through it. But small is the gate and narrow the road that leads to life, and only a few find it," (Matthew 7, 13–14). The message of a God-dream will always reflect God's character as revealed in Jesus. God's words bring peace and understanding in order to produce the fruit of the Spirit or Godly character in you and to keep you close to the Father. Jesus is the good shepherd, preventing you from wandering off the narrow path. His is not a voice of condemnation but of loving conviction.

God can tell you about world events and show you what is going on in the spiritual realms

My daughter had a dream of great national importance. She is a generation Z Esther type, very bold in her community which includes all sorts of identifications. Some months before the queen died on 8th September 2022, she had the following dream:

"I dreamt I was coming home across the bridge with Mum and my younger brothers. The cars in front and behind us suddenly stopped. All the lights had gone out. People got out of, and abandoned their cars. Mum asked a guy in a little green Fiat what was going on. He was old, grey haired with a long beard. He said: "The Queen has died and the regiment is leaving."'

This dream was a dream of national spiritual importance and a call to national prayer given the Holy Spirit—'the old grey wise man'—had warned that the angelic covering over the UK, given the godly queen's presence—'the regiment'—was leaving, given the queen was a true believer. I looked up the word 'Fiat.' In a dream you can't just accept that the car was a green Italian car and think 'groovy car.' Which frankly I did, but of course I then mined for more information. Green in this context is symbolic of newness or fresh wisdom or revelation. 'Fiat' in Latin, means 'let it be done,' it is used when issuing a decree by someone in great authority. The Cambridge Dictionary terms it: "the giving of orders by someone who has complete authority," ie. God. To anyone living in the UK now with 'ears to hear and eyes to see,' the undermining of the Christian constitution in this country that is based on the monarch who is head of the church of England and head of state is being eroded. In essence, the monarch is the root of our Christian constitution that has now been pulled up. We now have a King with questionable Christian beliefs, and an heir who does not want to be head of the church, or so the press reports. The spiritual protection has been removed and all hell has broken loose on our streets. We see Islam rapidly taking the place of Christianity in this country and given the free rein that Christianity no longer has. For example, Christians can be arrested for publicly praying, even silently but adherents of Islam are afforded

107

comparative respect. Islamic prayer was held *en masse* outside the prime minister's residence in London to protest the Gaza hospital compound bombing that was was blamed on Israel. The gathering shut down traffic on Whitehall a key London route. This sends a clear symbolic message. Freedom of religion and expression should be a fundamental right for all, but Christianity is increasingly not tolerated in this arguably former Christian country; the irony being that our Christian laws give those freedoms in the first place.

God can warn about satanic agenda in Government Policy

"For God speaks again and again, though people do not recognise it. He speaks in dreams, in visions of the night, when deep sleep falls on people as they lie in their beds. He whispers in their ears and terrifies them with warnings. He makes them turn from doing wrong; He keeps them from pride. He protects them from the grave, from crossing over the river of death... Behold, God does all these oftentimes with men, to bring back his soul from the pit, that he may be enlightened with the light of life." (Job 33:14–18, 29–30).
God can show you demonic agendas to wake you up and get you to intercede to frustrate the plans of the enemy!

I dreamed of a large and hideous transgender demon with huge grey leathery wings and gauzy ripped very short dress, very apparently male but with garish make up over his darkly shaved face. He tried to shove me into a cupboard. I was warned he was coming after 'my children.'

In the dream I as a woman and mother represented the church. The high ranking demon, was from the principality that had been sent to the UK to influence policy at ground level. As I sat in bed with my dream journal pondering the dream, my husband came in with a newspaper advertising *The Family Sex Show*—a show for families with children as young as 5 to go to so they can see adults naked and speaking about various forms of sex including transgender sex. I got on the phone to intercessors and began to intercede, as I am sure many others did. The show was cancelled but the personification of the principality I saw is already in policy and in schools in Wales and all over the UK. This demon has been after the children in the church and children in general. Heartbreakingly I have seen the agenda take root and take some of our Christian children. There is Biblical precedent for being able to see into satanic agendas: 'Dark Dreams' if you like. God 'discussed' hideous demonic acts with and through Jeremiah that were taking place in Israel when God asked him to pronounce judgement for their following "worthless idols," and indulging in child sacrifice and the like.

God can warn of impending disaster in order to avert it

We previously mentioned how God frightened Abimelech half to death in a dream by night and said to him, "Behold, you are a dead man because of the woman whom you have taken, for she is a man's wife." Genesis 20:3 ESV Here we see God warning Abimelech that unless he caught a massive wake up he'd be a dead man for taking Abram's wife even though he thought she was his sister. Abram's daft plan did not exactly work out. Needless to say, after remonstrating with God, Abimelech jumped around to rectify matters and the course of the history of God's people progressed along Godly lines.

Ward Hill Lamon, an aide to President Lincoln, claimed he was one of two or three people present when Lincoln told him about a dream he had shortly before it came to pass.

"In this account, Lincoln began by commenting on the abundance of dreams in the Bible and asserting, "If we believe the Bible, we must accept the fact that in the old days God and His angels came to men in their sleep and made themselves known in dreams." In answer to a question put to him by his wife, Lincoln admitted that he did not believe in dreams, but he went on nevertheless to allude to a recent dream that "has haunted me ever since." Prodded by Mrs. Lincoln to continue, the president related that "about ten days ago" he had gone to bed late after he had stayed up "waiting for important dispatches from the front." As he began to dream, he experienced "a death-like stillness about me." Hearing the sounds of subdued sobs, Lincoln walked downstairs in search of the "mournful sounds of distress," but encountered no living person until he entered the East Room, where he found "a sickening surprise": a covered corpse resting on a catafalque, surrounded by soldiers, with mourners gazing at the body and weeping. "'Who is dead in the White House?' I demanded of one of the soldiers," Lincoln related in Lamon's account, continuing, "'The President,' was his answer; 'he was killed by an assassin!'" Lincoln then stated that he awoke soon after in response to a "loud burst of grief from the crowd," did not sleep again that night due to the dream, and "have been strangely annoyed by it since."

There are lots of incidences in the Bible where God warned His people of impending disaster, often through angels, angels of the Lord, or Himself in some way. One night around 2004 I came out of sleep in the morning, I had been dreaming of an earthquake with people crying and standing on piles of rubble. I knew the application of the dream was to pray. Later the news told me of a massive earthquake in Turkey.

God can heal you and comfort you in dreams

God can heal us in dreams. Often this is the way he most commonly heal us. It's in the maker's programming to heal when we are asleep. How many times have you prayed for healing, gone to bed, and woken healed? He can do this emotionally and physically.

God repeatedly tries to save your life in dreams

A few years before I was diagnosed, I had a dream in which I went for a medical check up at a hospital. I was laughing and joking until medical staff told me they wanted to 'check for lumps.' I did not take them seriously until the showed me a bell shape with two thin winged area onto which the lumps were growing. This was a picture of the uterus and ovaries. Both of which needed to be removed a few years later when in 2018 it was discovered that I had ovarian cancer for which I needed extensive surgery.

God showed me the BRCA gene

It was 2016. My mother was dying. I was going through an *annus horribilis* as the queen might have put it. Much else was coming against us. The stress was real, but God continued to train me even harder in the tough seasons. I really had to lean on Him and it was a time where faith and hope were all I had to hold on to. But it was about to get much, much worse in the next two years, but by the end of this season, I really knew that I was an overcomer by the blood of the lamb. One night I had a dream in which I saw a syringe filled with dark blood. I knew that God was speaking to me about an issue with blood. I was soon to have breast surgery for a lump that was full of infected blood, but if I knew then what I know now, I would have pressed in more for further information. When I had ovarian cancer, I insisted that medical staff run some tests to see what was happening genetically. I had previously repeatedly asked for this and if they had found it earlier I may not have had to go through a life threatening situation and 6 months of chemotherapy, but even in the build up to discovery, God kept bugging me to get checked until He gave me two massive pain episodes and a blood issue that had me running to the emergency room, where they missed my symptoms twice as the symptoms I had only reveal themselves in the final phase of ovarian cancer and I was in the first, treatable phase. Finally, on the third symptom, they found the issue of the blood. I was later to be found to be a carrier of the BRCA 1 gene—this was the 'bad blood.' At the risk of revealing my entire medical history, here's one more!

God told me to eat beans

You are described in the Bible as "a temple of the Holy Spirit." God cares about your bodily health. I was suffering from an ongoing digestive issue when I had a dream about going into a doctor's surgery. The doctor, a woman, told me to eat beans. When I began eating beans, the issue went away. In this dream the doctor is a type of the Holy Spirit or messenger of the Lord. The surgery is the heavenly healing room we all have access to.

God can give you specific direction in dreams

God has repeatedly given us as a family direction in dreams as to where we are to move to. In Genesis 31:10-13, we see Jacob move to the land of his relative Laban, where he marries Laban's daughters and works with his herds. Laban tricks Jacob and takes advantage of Jacob on several occasions, but God still provides for Jacob—so much so that Jacob's wealth begins to overtake Laban's which causes jealousy. God comes to Jacob in a dream. The dream recaps Laban's mistreatment of Jacob and shows that God has been providing for Jacob despite Laban's dodgy behaviour. The dream's message is clear: it is time for Jacob to return home and he will do so, wealthier than ever, and with his bride of choice and the sister he didn't want in the first place.

Someone close to me was applying for universities. He did not consider his *alma mater* as it was no longer local and he did not think they ran the course he was looking to do. God gave him a dream where a card was handed to him with the name of his *alma mater* on it. When he googled it he saw it was one of the best in the country for his field. He applied, and was accepted.

God can show you your long term destiny in Dreams

God showed Jacob his plan for Israel and the redemption of mankind through the blessing of the Messiah. "There above it stood the Lord, and he said: "I am the Lord, the God of your father Abraham and the God of Isaac. I will give you and your descendants the land on which you are lying. Your descendants will be like the dust of the earth, and you will spread out to the west and to the east, to the north and to the south. All peoples on earth will be blessed through you and your offspring," (Genesis 28, 13–14). I have had many 'calling' dreams and visions, some of which have already come to pass and some I wait for in anticipation and prayer. Joseph's destiny dreams that we have already looked at (the sheaves and stars bowing down to him) that may well have sustained him through his slavery and prison seasons.

God can give you gifts of the Holy Spirit in Dreams

"At Gibeon the Lord appeared to Solomon in a dream by night, and God said, "Ask what I shall give you." (1 Kings 3:5 ESV). God gave wisdom to Solomon in a dream and He can impart gifts to you in your dreams. How often have you asked God for wisdom in a situation only to receive it in a dream, but perhaps you have not recognised it? And then you think God has not answered your prayer!

God can give you direction on your work or calling

If you dream of a jumbo jet or a large white ship, this could mean a big ministry call on your life. If the plane is grounded or there is a delay taking off, there may be some training or character issues God needs to deal with before take off. There may be issues with the pilot—the boss or pastor. She might need some prayer so that the wind of the spirit can get that bird in the air! If there is turbulence, you are perhaps being warned about trouble in your church or in your company, depending on who is in your plane or 'on your plane' work wise or in the context of your dream. God tends to pun a lot with me, but then I appreciate wordplay. If you have lost your passport more than once God is likely highlighting areas you need to be prepared for before He can take you to the next phase of your journey. A bicycle is made for you only, no one else is on that ride with you unless it's a bicycle made for two. Vehicles in dreams symbolise your means of getting somewhere in your journey through life, or your spiritual journey. Consider the nature of the vehicle as being aligned to *purpose.* Is it going too fast? Too slow? Is something blocking or hindering its/your progress? Similarly your life needs to be on track for a train journey with various carriages or episodes en route. A train can be a 'training' or a 'train of thought.' Train tracks can show that you are 'on track' or off it if the tracks are broken. Consider the colour, size and speed of the vehicle and what cultural groups tend to use that colour make or size of vehicle. In 2022/23, God gave me a number of visions through other prophets on the teaching, coaching and writing I am currently doing and the 'vehicles' necessary to get me there—not cars but digital resource vehicles such as computers. Context is everything with symbols.

God cares about your every day life

We have been restoring a building with little funds. We needed a kitchen and were thinking of trying to find second hand components. My husband had a dream about a local bespoke kitchen company that ordinarily we would not be able to afford. In the dream, we were in the carpark outside the kitchen place "Oh come on, let's go and have a look." A day or so later we were driving along the motorway and a sign for this kitchen company was on a lorry we were overtaking stating that we could pay the kitchen off over 6 months interest free, so that we could afford the repayments. God even cares about how good our kitchens look and function!

God can show you how He is promoting you or elevating you spiritually

When God is promoting spiritually or upping your training you may find you can fly and soar without wings or take great supernaturally high leaps across lawns, hilltops and mountaintops. These dreams are exciting and exhilarating and you never want to wake up from them. If you are a prophet you may dream you are able to look directly into the sun with your extraordinary yellow eye. This is a dream about deep prophetic insight, as one who can commune deeply with the Father of Lights—God. You may find yourself going up in an elevator with significant numbers being highlighted: potentially an image of promotion, or being 'elevated' in the spirit. If you are walking upstairs with effort, a season of training may be required! Going downstairs can be to do with the past.

God can give you creative ideas in your dreams

I often receive creative ideas for novels, songs (even melodies), and paintings via a process of daydreaming and sometimes in dreams at night— particularly for my visual art pieces, which I quickly sketch into an art journal. Dreams have been the progenitors of famous films and books: William Styron's *Sophie's Choice* came to him in the twilight zone before waking and sleeping: "One morning in the early spring, I woke up with the remembrance of a girl I'd once known, Sophie. It was a very vivid half-dream, half-revelation, and all of a sudden I realised that hers was a story I had to tell." The idea for the film *The Terminator* came to the director and co-writer of the film, James Cameron through a nightmare. "The Terminator came from a dream that I had while I was sick with a fever in a cheap *pensione* in Rome in 1981. It was the image of a chrome skeleton emerging from a fire. When I woke up, I began sketching on the hotel stationery." (Interview from BFI, The British Film Institute, 21 April 2021).

God can give you business and work solutions in dreams

Jacob was given a business strategy regarding goats. He ended up being a very successful man indeed! (Genesis 30:25). Incidentally, this method of breeding has now been proved to be a valid method of breeding due to modern research methods. It's amazing how much knowledge God gave the ancient Jews to survive as well as they did in a hostile world, from fasting on a vegan diet, to not eating pork that quickly contaminates without refrigeration; or three day water fasts as seen with the prophet Daniel and Queen Esther to the hygiene and dietary practises of the Jews, that prevented disease, to Joseph's political strategies for surviving natural disasters, to the renewing of the plasticity of the mind in the New Testament. The Bible had it first, people!

Before Helena Rubenstein or Kylie ever became cosmetic millionaires, Madam C.J Walker, a former slave and laundress, became the first African American self made millionaire. After losing her hair she embarked on a determined discovery to find a cure. Walker credited God with giving her the formula for her hair growth solution in a dream: *"God answered my prayer, for one night I had a dream, and in that dream a big Black man appeared to me and told me what to mix up for my hair. Some of the remedy was grown in Africa, but I sent for it, mixed it, put it on my scalp, and in a few weeks my hair was coming in faster than it had ever fallen out. I tried it on my friends; it helped them. I made up my mind I would begin to sell it."* She was a talented marketeer, but had she not had the solution to the problem, in both senses, she would have been nothing but a snake oil saleswoman[8].

Dmitri Mendelev, inventor of the periodic table, recognised a pattern in the elements and was convinced he was close to a breakthrough. In a dream, he saw the table of elements, perfectly formed. He wrote it down as soon as he woke up. Although there were some changes that were made later, the table as it is today is much the same as the one that came in the dream.

Einstein's Theory of Relativity is reported to have come to him in a dream. In a dream Einstein walked through a farm when he saw cows by an electric fence. As the fence gave them an electric shock, he observed the cows jump at the same time. However, a farmer, standing at the other end of the field, saw them jump one by one, like a Mexican wave. Einstein realised views of the same event were relative to the position the observer was standing in because of the time it takes for the light to reach your eyes.

In the 18th Century after a dream about a snake biting its tail, the inventor of benzene, August Kekulé realised that the snake in his dream was a structural representation of a benzene molecule. Hitherto this structure was unlike anything else in chemistry.
Dr James Watson saw a spiral staircase in a dream in 1953, which led to the idea of a double helix spiral structure for our DNA. Watson went on to win the Nobel Prize in Physiology or Medicine in 1962. All thanks to a recognisable dream that was heeded!

---

[8] https://www.biography.com/inventors/madam-cj-walker-invent-hair-care-products

God can keep you sane through dreams

God knew what He was doing when He designed the mystery of sleeping. According to the National Library of Medicine, "In otherwise healthy adults, short-term consequences of sleep disruption include increased stress responsivity, somatic pain, reduced quality of life, emotional distress and mood disorders, and cognitive, memory, and performance deficits." New mothers know how crazy they can begin to feel when sleep deprived. We dream for an hour or two every night. We need to sleep for our emotional health. If we suffer from a lack of sleep we can get depressed and even delusional. If people are repeatedly woken during REM sleep, they begin to show symptoms of madness. God made us to sleep healing, refreshing sleep and to dream! During REM sleep, our inner and outer eyes move. Our eyes are literally moving as we watch our dreams! In 2015 an international team of researchers led by UCLA's Dr. Itzhak Fried in association with Israeli researchers in Tel Aviv discovered that "Brain cells in the medial temporal lobe showed a sudden surge of activity each time after patients moved their eye in REM sleep. This electrical pattern closely resembles what happens when we view something new in waking life. We suspect rapid eye movements reflect the instant when the brain encounters a new image in a dream." The finding implies that rapid eye movement captures snapshots of dream imagery, suggesting that the same machinery that informs our conscious visual experience also operates during sleep." Why would we want to miss out on God doing a new thing when we sleep? "See, I am doing a new thing! Now it springs up; do you not perceive it? I am making a way in the wilderness and streams in the wasteland," (Isaiah 43:19)

Chapter 10. We are Required to Interpret Dreams and not Translate them

"We both had dreams," they replied, "but there is no one to interpret them." Then Joseph said to them, "Don't interpretations belong to God? Tell me your dreams."
Genesis 40:8

The Bible

Lawyers in the UK have this big white book of civil procedure that legal professionals adhere to. Literature scholars have *The Complete Works of Shakespeare* amongst other books. Believers have the Bible, God's other gift to us apart from Jesus: our manual for life and living—and for dream interpretation. This is our primary text and if you take shortcuts you will be short cut! I can't stress this enough. You need to know God and how He speaks and you need to know the Bible to interpret dreams correctly. These are the foundational principles and they are non negotiable. God is the dream creator and giver and he made you with the capacities to receive and interpret dreams for yourself—certainly the ones that are personal to you—which is almost all of them. "The words which I have spoke to you are spirit and are life," (John 6:63). Ephesians 5:26 says: "That He might sanctify her, (the Church) cleansing her by the washing of the water in the word." This is the kind of word coming to us, that 'washes over us,' and can have a dramatic affect on our spiritual lives. A word that comes at just the right time and applies to your current life circumstances. It has connotations of 'revealed.' I usually receive a *rhema* word that backs up a dream I have or an interpretation for another person.

"The Word became flesh and made his dwelling among us. We have seen his glory, the glory of the one and only Son, who came from the Father, full of grace and truth." (John 1:14). Jesus encapsulates all of the elements of the word as He is the living truth available to us through the Holy Spirit and all the wisdom or dream solution we need. You do not need a dream encyclopaedia or ten compiled by non Biblical writers: they do not reveal God's *rhema* word for you. God reveals his personal word to you through the secret message of your dream. You will be compiling your own 'encyclopaedia' or dictionary and I will show you how to do that. The reason Jesus spoke in parables was because he was 'preaching to the converted,' in a manner of speaking. The wisdom he was giving was for believers or those who would come to believe. Not for the *hoi poloi*—the masses. It was to believers with 'eyes to see and ears to hear' that Jesus gave the keys of knowledge to. It is no different today. First and foremost you need to be an actual follower of Jesus. Which means knowing Him intimately, not just knowing 'of Him.' You get to know Him much the same as you get to know anyone else. Through talking to Him and waiting to hear Him reply —not just talking at Him in or of Him, or reciting lists to Him. This is no way to conduct a relationship, or anything actually. One way traffic it is not. We learn to hear Him replying through the word of God—*rhema* —coming into your mind when you are seeking answers, or by 'the still quiet voice' that Elijah heard in 1 Kings19:12: "After the earthquake came a fire, but the LORD was not in the fire. And after the fire came a gentle whisper." Or through a timely word via a friend. When you have asked you will receive, one way or the other, and so it is with dreams, as long as we ask with the right intentions and motives. Being a disciple or follower of Jesus is different to 'being saved' or having heard the gospel, and thereby welcoming Jesus into your life. We need to embark on a developing, deepening and growing relationship with Him. We need to know Him in the Biblical sense! Deeply and intimately. The Bible tells us in Psalm 23 that Jesus 'the Lord' is our shepherd. We are likened to sheep who 'lie down in green pastures.' Green is the colour of health, but for me, it is often the colour of wisdom, it can also mean new life or a fresh perspective. Sheep feed on fresh green grass, this is the 'manna' from heaven for them. Jesus is our best and most vital source of nourishment, but how many believers will spend hours listening to second hand regurgitated knowledge fed to them by video by those who make a living from selling messages? Like baby birds with their gullets exposed many of these will swallow anything particular ministries peddle to them—books, teaching series', hoodies, notebooks. Mugs. You name it (these items aren't necessarily wrong, I like mugs! But you get the point). If it's branded they'll buy it. It's Disneyland out there and as believers we need to be discerning. There are platform ministries with teachers and prophets I greatly respect and enjoy being taught by, but if I'm going to spend a lot of time reading a book, I need to respect the ministry, discern that their messages are 'well sourced' as in, revelation from God for the body of Christ today. CS Lewis and Derek Prince are people I return to over and over again. There are not many like them, but the Bible was their primary text and it should be yours and mine too. Be discerning. The Bible tells us "we have the mind of Christ. "Therefore use it strategically and with discernment. Seek God first. Not someone else. He will add to your learning all you need. "But seek first his kingdom and his righteousness, and all these things will be given to you as well" (Matthew 6:33).

Learning from the Bible

How to decode dreams using the bible— Nebuchadnezzar's dream

In Psalm 119:105, the Bible tells us that the "Your word is a lamp for my feet, a light on my path.' In terms of hearing for dreams and visions, it really is all the read we need.

The Bible is the best book ever! The wisdom to be found in its pages is second to none. There is plenty of other wisdom in the world and I would not dismiss all of it. I have studied Psychology, Theology, Literature and Psychoanalysis and have gained plenty of insight, knowledge and wisdom from these methodologies, and continue to do so but there is nothing like drinking the pure clean water from the *font* of wisdom and knowledge Himself: God. I see dreams as a supernatural highway between us and God's eternal kingdom. We are already situated in the eternal kingdom in that when we accepted Christ into our lives this kingdom became a part of us. Eternity is not time bound. In a way then, we have the opportunity to engage with visits to our eternal home nightly! Or live symbiotically between two kingdoms: earth and heaven. God communes directly with our spirits through dreams. "What is mankind that you make so much of them, that you give them so much attention, that you examine them every morning and test them every moment?" (Job 7:18–19). In the book of Job we are told that God visits every morning like a postman. I find I am dreaming most vividly or memorably, when I am just about to wake up. This is God's grace. If he did not operate like this we'd be likely to forget the dreams we are given. Sometimes He wakes me in the night so that I can note down the episodes of dreaming I receive then. The best way to begin training in dream interpretation is to begin to write down all your dreams however opaque or baffling they might seem or however fragmented. As you are faithful in doing so, God will give you more. This process is like passing a series of heavenly exams. The more you pass, the more you get. Before you begin to do so, acknowledge the dream giver and give glory to God, as Daniel did: "Then begin to jot down the symbols in the dream as Daniel also did: "In the first year of Belshazzar king of Babylon, Daniel had a dream, and visions passed through his mind as he was lying in bed. He wrote down the *substance* of his dream," (Daniel 7:1). Once you have written down, or cracked the code of the dream, an interpretation should soon emerge. Pray and mull over this interpretation and ask God for further wisdom. You may not get all the interpretation at once, but don't worry, Daniel sometimes mulled and prayed over his dreams for weeks. Such was the stunning nature of his foretelling dreams, dreams of great national and historic importance, that he had to lie down in a dark room to nurse his headaches (Daniel 2:24–49). When you have the interpretation for yourself or others, give glory to God! "Praise be to the name of God for ever and ever; wisdom and power are his. He changes times and seasons; he deposes kings and raises up others. He gives wisdom to the wise, and knowledge to the discerning. He reveals deep and hidden things; he knows what lies in darkness, and light dwells with him. I thank and praise you, God of my ancestors: You have given me wisdom and power, you have made known to me what we asked of you, you have made known to us the dream of the king." (Daniel 2, 20–23).

Let's look closely at one of Daniel's dreams to see how to interpret a dream biblically. The text in bold highlights the symbols and important statements and the interpretation of the symbols and my comments/ thinking are in italics. "Then Daniel went to Arioch, whom the king had appointed to execute the wise men of Babylon, and said to him, 'Do not execute the wise men of Babylon. Take me to the king, and I will interpret his dream for him.'—*Daniel already has a good reputation at court. Here we see him exhibiting his wisdom and tact. The King was so disturbed by the power of his dream that he was threatening to kill all the wise men unless he got an interpretation, but Daniel thought calmly, rationally, and with wisdom, which is how he approached Arioch.* "Arioch took Daniel to the king at once" *He didn't want to die!* and said, "I have found a man among the exiles from Judah who can tell the king what his dream means." *We can infer that he likely also wanted to curry favour with the king by bringing him good news.* The king asked Daniel, 'Are you able to tell me what I saw in my dream and interpret it?' *Daniel had not even heard the dream but knew he knew he could interpret it with God's help.* Daniel replied, "No wise man, enchanter, magician or diviner can explain to the king the mystery he has asked about, but there is a God in heaven who reveals mysteries." *Daniel gives the glory to God* **He has shown King Nebuchadnezzar what will happen in days to come.** Your dream and the visions that passed through your mind as you were lying in bed are these: 'As Your Majesty was lying there, your mind **turned to things to come** *this is a foretelling dream,* and the revealer of mysteries showed you what is going to happen. As for me, this mystery has been revealed to me, not because I have greater wisdom than anyone else alive, *though he probably did given his wisdom from God, but he was a humble man, which was why God exulted him to high station* but so that *Your Majesty* may know the interpretation and that you may understand what went through your mind. '*Your Majesty* looked, *he gives the King the honour of his position by acknowledging his status* and there before you stood a large statue—an enormous, dazzling statue, awesome in appearance *(he doesn't spare the details!).* **The**

head of the statue was made of pure gold *(synonymous with the great wealth of the Babylonian empire)*, **its chest and arms of silver** *(similar to gold but less valuable or important—symbolic of value/ money/transaction—but also, as we see in the later book of Ezra, articles of gold and silver were ransacked from God's temple were to be returned—see also the writing on the wall that appeared after the king and his courtiers used the stolen goblets from the temple to swig wine out of that the King's son later saw that incurred God's wrath)*, **its belly and thighs of bronze, its legs of iron,** *(stability and strength)* **its feet partly of iron** *(strength)* **and partly of baked clay** *(the earth)*. *These are the various Babylonian Kingdoms/Kingdoms of the earth, varying in power and strength.* While you were watching, a rock was cut out, **but not by human hands.** *This is God* It struck the statue on its feet of iron and clay and smashed them. Then the iron, the clay, the bronze, the silver and the **gold** *(Nebachudnezzar's Kingdom)* were all broken to pieces and became like chaff on a threshing-floor in the summer. *God causes empires to rise and fall. The wind = the Holy Spirit/power of God* —swept them away without leaving a trace. **But the rock that struck the statue became a huge mountain and filled the whole earth** *This is the coming Kingdom of God.* "This was the dream, and now we will interpret it to the king. Your Majesty, you are the king of kings. **The God of heaven has given you dominion and power and might and glory; in your hands he has placed all mankind and the beasts of the field and the birds in the sky** *(an echo of the tree dream/reminiscent of the King's other dream where he is represented as a tree—the carrying over of a theme or message)*. **Wherever they live, he has made you ruler over them all. You are that head of gold. After you, another kingdom will arise, inferior to yours. Next, a third kingdom, one of bronze, will rule over the whole earth. Finally,**

there will be a fourth kingdom, strong as iron—
for iron breaks and smashes everything—and as
iron breaks things to pieces, so it will crush and
break all the others. Just as you saw that the feet
(carry the person/bring good news as well as bad) **and
toes** *(balance)* **were partly of baked clay and partly
of iron, so this will be a divided kingdom; yet it
will have some of the strength of iron in it, even as
you saw iron mixed with clay. As the toes** *(balance)*
were partly iron and partly clay *(a mix),* **so this
kingdom will be partly strong and partly brittle.
And just as you saw the iron mixed with baked
clay, so the people will be a mixture and will not
remain united, any more than iron mixes with
clay. In the time of those kings, the God of heaven
will set up a kingdom that will never be
destroyed, nor will it be left to another people. It
will crush all those kingdoms and bring them to
an end, but it will itself endure for ever.** *(The
Kingdom of Heaven)* **This is the meaning of the
vision of the rock cut out of a mountain, but not
by human hands** *(by God's hands)* **—a rock that
broke the iron, the bronze, the clay, the silver and
the gold to pieces.**
'The great God *(the one and only triune, Judeo/
Christian God)* **has shown the king what will take
place in the future. The dream is true and its
interpretation is trustworthy.'** *(Of course it was
revealed by the 'revealer of mysteries: God)* Then King
Nebuchadnezzar fell prostrate before Daniel and paid
him honour and ordered that an offering and incense
be presented to him. The king said to Daniel, 'Surely
your God is the God of gods and the Lord of kings and
a revealer of mysteries, for you were able to reveal
this mystery.'
Then the king placed Daniel in a high position and
*lavished many gifts on him. (This is not the same as
'being paid,' elsewhere Daniel makes it clear he should
not be paid specifically, to interpret.)* He made him

ruler over the entire province of Babylon and placed him in charge of all its wise men. *(Here we see Godly promotion—not worldly promotion—that takes place in the context of faithful obedience)* Moreover, at Daniel's request the king appointed Shadrach, Meshach and Abednego chief ministers over the province of Babylon, while Daniel himself remained at the royal court. *(God rewarded Daniel through the King.)*

Previously, God used a vast tree as a symbol for the king and his power and dominion. He showed the root being cut off and chained to the earth as the king would be if he didn't heed the warning of the dream —which he didn't. Remember he can and will use different symbols at different times to symbolise people or events, as in the case of Joseph's dreams. And ours!

Chapter 11. Biblical Parables

Why Jesus speaks in parables

Jesus' disciples came and said to him, "Why do you use parables when you speak to the crowds?" Jesus replied, "Because they haven't received the secrets of the kingdom of heaven, but you have. For those who have will receive more and they will have more than enough. But as for those who don't have, even the little they have will be taken away from them. This is why I speak to the crowds in parables: although they see, they don't really see; and although they hear, they don't really hear or understand. What Isaiah prophesied has become completely true for them: You will hear, to be sure, but never understand; and you will certainly see but never recognise what you are seeing. For this people's senses have become calloused, and they've become hard of hearing, and they've shut their eyes so that they won't see with their eyes or hear with their ears or understand with their minds, and change their hearts and lives that I may heal them.

"Happy are your eyes because they see. Happy are your ears because they hear. I assure you that many prophets and righteous people wanted to see what you see and hear what you hear, but they didn't."
Matthew 13:10–17

Jesus is a master artist; his language is creative and visual, and carries resonance and depth of meaning that prosaic language does not. A parable is a memorable short story glimmering with metaphors, or symbols, that carry great truth and wisdom for life. Jesus sought us out and purchased us with His blood. He desires to communicate with us through His intimate love language as illustrated by parables and in dream symbolism. As He has first sought us out, (Luke 19:10) let us seek Him with all our hearts in return and learn His language as fluently as we can. We have everything to gain. Some might ask, 'Why does He not just communicate with us directly.' He does, through literal dreams, but I'd argue that symbolic language is also direct: it is from His heart to ours. He wants to be known by us; to be experienced by us. Jesus's visual language is memorable. We remember stories, music and poetry where we often forget conversations.

The mysterious process of a picture from life being revealed through traditional photographic development is a marvellous metaphor for the dream interpretation process.

I had a good friend at art school who was a fantastic photographer. We often did photographic shoots at her flat in Johannesburg where her father had given her a room to use as a darkroom. The process of developing a negative into a photograph is full of useful symbolism to illustrate the process of dream interpretation. I recall the warm womb like glow of the room bathed as it was in the the red safety light, full of creative possibility. From choosing an old fashioned negative from a sheet (symbolic of an uncoded dream) to placing it in a tray (you = container of the revelation) and bathing it in developer solution (the Holy Spirit = dream solver), to watching the colour photograph emerge (decoding the dream) before hanging up to dry on a line (seeing if it 'lines up' with the Word) to the grand finale of the photograph being framed (applying the dream to the framework or context of one's life). I may not have remembered a conversation about photography, but I remember the story of the experience, the imagery of the above process.

Let's look at one of Jesus' parables. I have highlighted the symbols and their meanings in bold.

The Parable of the Sower (Matthew 13:1–9)

On that day Jesus went out of the house and was sitting by the **sea (synonymous with the world)**. And large crowds gathered close around him, so that he got into a **boat (taking us on a narrative journey)** to sit down, and all the crowd **(believers to be and non believers)** was standing on the shore **(place of possibility/taking off)** . And he spoke many things to them in parables, saying, "Behold, the **sower (God)** went out to **sow, (the truth/gospel)** and while he was **sowing**, some **seed (seeds of eternal life)** fell on the side of the path, **(the route to God)** and the **birds (demons/snatchers of truth)** came and **devoured (the destroyer/satan)** it. And other seed fell on the **rocky ground (person who initially receives the word but is then distracted or turns from it as there is no depth/they are 'untillable'—sic)**, where it did not have much **soil**, and it sprang up at once because it did not have any **depth** of soil. But when the **sun rose it was scorched (hard times or persecution)**, and because it did not have enough **root**, it **withered (died)**. And other seed fell among the **thorn plants (The message of truth or gospel is heard, but people's concern for riches and their worries about life cause the plants to choke and die)** and the thorn plants came up and **choked (stifled it of killed it)** it. But other **(believers)** seed fell on the **good soil (people who receive, act and live out of the word of God)** and produced **grain (life giving fruit/character)**, this one a hundred times **(eternal truth)** as much and this one **sixty** and this one **thirty (the gift that keeps on giving is lived out of!)** The one who has **(spiritual)** ears, let him hear **(through the spirit)**!"

In order to demonstrate symbology and how symbols function, I've written another parable for you to decode. Write the symbols and symbolic phrases (in bold) down. Then write possible meanings next to them. Then decide what the hidden message of the dream is. After you have written out the dreams code, consider whether any of the symbolic language resonates with scriptures. Write them down too. The dream key for this parable can be found at the end of the book.

Parable of the lost daughter

A young woman called Joanna, grew up in a village in an **adopted** country in Western Europe. She had been living there with her mother after a **war** in her **home** country in the **Middle East** ripped her **family** apart. Her **father**, who went off to **fight in the war** did not return and after some years of waiting in vain, Joanna and her mother **emigrated.** Despite her mother's love, Joanna grew up longing for her father. Across the road from her **office** was a little **park** where Joanna would go during her **lunch break.** She would sit and look at the **beautiful coloured birds** that flocked there, **marvelling at their magnificence and their diversity**. Often an **old man** would be there, **a traveller, passing through. The birds seemed to love him and would feed from his hands.** Joanna was curious and **wanted to feed the birds too.** The man showed her how to reach out to them gently so that they would not be afraid and soon they began to feed out of her hands as well. Sometimes Joanna and the man would have simple conversations, about the weather, about the birds, or the **countries** he had been to. Afterwards, Joanna found that **his words**

132

remained in her, taking flight like the birds and landing in her heart. The words he spoke seemed to have various meanings, **pointing her, in her thought life, to particular areas and situations.** Joanna enjoyed speaking to him, he was **mysterious, yet somehow familiar.** Soon Joanna was promoted in her job and met a young man who became her fiancée. She began **going to the park less and less.** Then the winter came and the snows fell and she did not visit the park for a **long time.** The old man would go to the park every day, in the hopes of seeing her and talking to her, even in the depths of winter. One day, news came to Joanna of an **inheritance** that she was to receive from her home country. She received the news from a **lawyer** who said that the relative who had arranged to give her the money was still living and would contact her around her birthday. The envelope she received the news in had a particular **old fashioned wax seal**, stamped with a **crown** and was from her **home country.** Joanna was very excited and as her **birthday** was coming up, she decided to prepare a **banquet** to which she would invite all the people of the village. She chose the best champagne, meat and vegetables, and ordered the finest linen, choicest crockery and silver cutlery for her table. **Word quickly spread of the inheritance and the party.** The old man too heard about the party and went to the park day after day in the **hopes** of seeing her and perhaps receiving an **invitation**. On the evening of the banquet he **dressed in his suit** and waited to see **if she would remember him** and invite him. At the **banquet**, Joanna sat down and looked at the glowing faces of her quests bathed in **candle light**, but despite the good cheer, she was **aware of a growing emptiness.** Even though there was **plenty, somehow there was lack.** Meanwhile the old man decided to go along to Joanna's house and look in at the **windows.** Just to see her enjoying herself would warm his heart. As Joanna sat down to eat, she **realised what was missing.** She rose, stating that she had forgotten something and that she would be back shortly. **Outside** the man **had begun to walk up the path to her door.** As she opened the door, the man was coming up the path, **she held out her hand** to him and he reached out for hers. As he did so, she noticed **a ring on his hand embedded with a crown.**

The parable is about God's longing to have relationship with us: to be in deep communion with us, even when we are unaware of His trying to engage with us—through our dreams for example; or when we reject Him in other ways: for the cares or the comforts of the world. He nevertheless always longs for communion with us.

Chapter 12. Skillset

The book of Proverbs tells us to search for wisdom above all things. Wisdom is a gift from God and knowledge is acquired. You will need both to interpret dreams. Sharpen your teeth—which can denote wisdom (wisdom teeth) by the way—on your dreams and you will become wiser and your bite sharper, metaphorically speaking! Daniel and Joseph were two of the wisest and cleverest men in the Bible. It is my belief that you become wiser and more like God the more you interpret dreams. Your brain and spirit get sharpened on the anvil of God's word and your 'iron'—humanity/being—gets sharpened on God's being—by being in the presence of the ultimate being you become a better human being in every way. What better sharpening could you acquire? The Bible tells us that "For the word of God is alive and active. Sharper than any double-edged sword, it penetrates even to dividing soul and spirit, joints and marrow; it judges the thoughts and attitudes of the heart," (Hebrews 4:12). How much sharper might we become if we sharpen ourselves nightly on the actual living rod—God, through dreams? How much better might we become in knowing ourselves and God's will for our lives? We, ourselves, are illuminated as we see ourselves reflected through the lens of God's eye. The mind boggles: this is God's invitation! But how many throw this invitation in the bin or ignore it, much less contemplate and apply it? Like most hard won or satisfying things, dream interpretation requires effort but the rewards are great, in both senses of the word! Train yourself in the visual language of heaven. It will make you more creative too! If you are seeing things through a dark prism, you may colour the dreams with your own thoughts. If you have a poor self image, you may draw the wrong conclusion, or a tendency to think negatively, your interpretation will 'keep you in the dark' as it were. Conversely, if you think too highly of yourself you may draw an inflated conclusion from the dream. It is God who brings balance and accuracy, and given he abhors 'dishonest' scales or a lack of balance, we need Him to punctuate the meaning. Ask God to illuminate your path with scripture, "Your word is a lamp for my feet, a light on my path," Psalm 119:105.

Developing Your Skillset

When I am decoding a dream, I know I am on the right path when a scripture to illustrate the interpretation comes into my head. This is Holy Spirit back up, or His stamp of approval to assure me that I am on the right track. The scripture will resonate or point up the meaning of the dream. These are the aspects of the word of God working in tandem: *logos* —context of the word of God coming to your brain or mind. *rhema*—the quickening of the revelation of a subjective word, relevant to the dream. This is important as it gives me biblical confirmation for my interpretation. Confirmation like this is important to keep you from getting wrong interpretations and being misguided. It's also why it's so important to know your Bible. Sometimes a favourite song or phrase from a movie or play will be flashed into my mind by the Holy Spirit. There is only one meaning to a dream, it is erroneous to think there is more than one meaning and it is important to keep mining your symbols until a clear message emerges. God may cloak things but He is not trying to be ambiguous. There is no biblical evidence of one dream being given more than one interpretation. God may give more than one dream with different symbols that point to the same meaning as with Pharaoh's dreams of the corn and then the cows, but both symbols lead to the same meaning. God is speaking to us and the circumstances of our lives very specifically and we need to 'search out the treasure with Him.' This searching leads to greater heights in the Lord God Almighty, or greater depths of understanding as we search for those pearls of wisdom. We often need to sit in the council of the Lord and not be flighty. Often the gist, or the outline of the dream will come in the first draft of the dream, but sometimes the dream will need to sit in the solution of the Holy Spirit for longer so that the picture emerges, particularly with corporate, national or international dreams. Write the whole vision down and note every detail and possible meaning. Pray over it. Take it out and swot it/study it over a period of days, weeks if necessary, if the dream still does not emerge keep a record of it. More dreams along the theme of the dream will come.

Make your own Dictionary

Begin to write down every dream and start your own dream dictionary at the back of your dream journal or in a separate book. For dreamers who want to get really serious, get a second A4 notebook or a series of small notebooks numbered A–Z to use as single letter dictionaries. Every time you have a dream and after you have decoded it, place each symbol with it's meaning, positive or negative in it's correct notebook or section. So in 'A' you might have alligator, aunt, apple and 'A' frame. If you like your aunt, put a plus sign for positive with the meaning. If your aunt was a passive aggressive nightmare of a woman (joke), put a negative symbol and the meaning—is she your actual aunt in the dream or is the dream highlighting a character trait of hers that is pertinent to you? Note it down. Note all positive and negative traits of the symbols. You might want to build your dictionary by category, with a section for clothes, colours, numbers, animals, parts of the body and vehicles for instance. In each category consider colour, culture, meaning and use. Don't forget directions (where symbols are north, south, left, right, up, down etc). Start with the Bible meanings and move on to personal, family or cultural meanings or representations of the symbol. If you want to develop this independently, you can do a Bible search per category. Over time you will build up your own non baffling skillset and you won't need to purchase a mind boggling tower of dream dictionaries. Alternatively, you can do this all digitally in files or just rely on the Holy Spirit each time.

Encyclopedias

We are required to interpret dreams and not translate them. Dream interpretation should not be undertaken without the Holy Spirit, 'the revealer of mysteries,' as He is described in the book of Daniel. I do not understand believers who will scoff down anything served up by pet ministries, be it book, teaching courses, conferences or YouTube videos, regardless of the calories or impact on the body of these unsifted teachings, but they spend no time 'chewing the fat' with God (mulling things over in the counsel of God) much less reading the Bible. People are like sheep, they really would follow some teachers or prophets over a cliff—many of whom I've had occasion to witness 'upfront and personal' or behind the scenes. Gifted as many are, they are as fallible to error as you or me and should not be slavishly followed. "Seek first the Kingdom of God and His righteousness and all these things will be given to you as well." Never settle for second best. You are a child of the king. You can go straight to his 'courts,' for counsel. Why go to a servant in the first instance? Go to Him first and the manual or primary text for dreams that He has given all of us—the Bible. This is his text. I studied English Literature, with Psychoanalysis at university for my first degree. There were set works of literature as well as books on Psychoanalysis, Philosophy and Postmodernism—a field of study alive with quacks, but that's another story. The point is we were required to read the texts supplied. If we wanted to read 'out of the box' or beyond these sources, of course we could but these texts were not supplied and neither were they *required.* Indeed some of these books might have led us down the wrong path in terms of what was required to pass a particular module. I'd be lying if I said I never looked at dream books. I acquired one when I was first learning, and according to the advice I was receiving at the time. Recently I acquired another on the recommendation of a ministry I am affiliated to. For the purposes of this book I acquired yet another and did a compare and contrast over a few of them. You're welcome. Many of the examples given are harmonious but some are completely different, which could become very confusing. Forsake MacDonalds for the King's table. Put the work in and spend time in the word of God and in the counsel of God, soon you will have your personal study or skillset applied to your dream. The quickening of the meaning will begin to come more automatically to your spirit—a personal word of God for your specific situation. God rewards a diligent student.

The problem with encyclopaedias is that every writer uses symbols that are meaningful to them whether these are biblical, cultural or personal. Symbols in dream dictionaries often have different meanings in different cultures, or are filtered through the writer's subjective prism. For example, if you have been attacked by a German Shepherd dog as a child (as I was), that dog might have negative connotations for you, particularly if it had poo on its paws when it leaped at you (mine did). But if a German Shepherd was your childhood companion, a German Shepherd will have good connotations for you. It could be a symbol of the Holy Spirit guiding and protecting you. Dogs can be holy or unholy, depending on your cultural or personal experiences. There is also no biblical precedent for dream encyclopaedias. Encyclopaedias are dependent on human wisdom and not on God's. They are impersonal—based on the writer's experience, though many have biblical references which you can look up online yourself. They can be confusing, involving as they often do, unfamiliar rhetoric or culturally specific symbolism. They can lead to error based on over reliance on a teacher rather than God. In short, be wary of the many books and dream encyclopaedias out there. If writer and dream course teachers are not using the Bible to teach you or are trying to sell you teaching materials or workshops with cunningly written esoteric sounding content or phrases ask the Holy Spirit first. If people seem to be selling themselves rather than the truth of God as revealed through the Bible, walk on by, as Whitney Houston's aunt so beautifully sang. Never forget that the enemy of your spirit aka satan is the author of confusion. God wants to speak to you directly and in a direct manner. There are so many people peddling their gifting and not all of them are good. Be discipled by Jesus! All the symbols you need are to be found in the Bible, the rest are to be found in your own culture—your country and society's customs and your own personal preferences. If God uses symbols He chooses them based on what they mean to you rather than someone else and for the setting and context of your particular, even *peculiar* dream. On the other hand, biblical symbols often point to a dream coming from God. If you insist on a dream dictionary make sure it's a Biblical one and cross reference with your own Bible or check if there are further meanings for your symbol in question.

Swot & Jot (the Bible dreams and parables)

By this, I mean do a search for and study all the dreams and and parables of the Bible. We are mostly familiar with the parables of Jesus if we are believers. It is really useful to study the biblical parables given your dreams are like Jesus speaking parables to you. What a gift. Make a list of all the symbols and their interpretations. List them in the dictionary you are compiling of biblical, personal and cultural symbols. If you are feeling ambitious. Write your own parable using some of the symbols you have learned and listed in your dream symbol dictionary. Do the same with your visions. Soon your brain will be adept at finding symbolic meaning quickly and easily, and you will be cleverer and more creative than you were before. Truly!

Google, Blue Study Bible, Online Bibles etc.

If you are not a student of the word and don't easily recall scripture, you may need to Google what your animals, people, teeth or feet mean in your dream. For example you can google: 'leopard' in the Bible, or 'teeth' in the Bible and reams of information will pop up for you to apply discernment to. There will be a number of references. The one (if it is there) that makes sense in the setting of your dream and context of your life will be the one the Holy Spirit highlights as you prayerfully search. Use a reputable site like Bible Study Tools, Bible Hub or Bible Gateway (biblehub.com, https://www.biblegateway.com/) for scripture. bible.com is another good one—

YouVersion. Bible Gateway has a list of 1670 symbols[9].

I really have given you all you need in terms of biblical resources but you still need God and the Holy Spirit to interpret and apply the dream. You will be equipped by the above and the other information in this book.

---

[9] https://www.biblegateway.com/resources/dictionary-of-bible-themes/1670-symbols

Chapter 13. Dreams are Personal

You might think that your strange dream was because of what you ate the night before or that freaky film you watched. I believe God uses the information we pick up during the day to speak to us, so don't dismiss the fact that information you saw the day before shows up in your dream, God will use that information to try to get through to us. God is relational. He is interested in what we are interested in. He will speak to us in ways that we understand, and through what we are interested in or through what is meaningful to us. Because I love literature, God speaks to me through books, poetry, Shakespeare and the language of the King James Bible. I have loved popular music since I was a small child, so snatches of songs across the decades may float into my mind when I am decoding, to punctuate or further illustrate meaning. The other day I saw a waterside rising (an unusually high spring tide) and God spoke to me through a song *The Tide is High* by the band *Blondie* to show me that my family and I would be moving on. This may sound crackers to some, but this is one of the most frequent ways that the Lord communicates with me, and it's how I know that God loves Elvis!

Subject, object

You are often the subject of your dream. The objects, the other elements in the dream, will be relational to you in some way. Sometimes someone or something else will be the subject or focus of the dream and the other elements the relational objects. The subject or main action of the dream—how the dream unfolds, will exert a pull on the objects of the dream. The outworking of which will be the interpretation of the dream that leads to the application of the dream taking place in your waking life. This is the dream's objective. Your dream's interpretation needs to be grounded in the setting of your dream world and then applied in the context of your own life. Consider the action you are to take, be it interceding or speaking to someone or getting counsel or deliverance, the bridge you take from the supernatural world of interaction into the the natural waking world of application. Some dreams are not to be shared but only prayed about between you and God only or with people he gives you leave to do so with.

Symbolism

A symbol is a thing that represents or stands for something else, often a concrete object representing something abstract. Symbolism uses objects, places, people, or ideas to represent something beyond their literal meaning. This is how a cow can become a symbol of famine and a star can become a brother, to borrow from Joseph's dreams. Symbolism is used to bring connection between characters, setting, and the action or events of the plot—as Jesus did with the parables. Symbols make sense in context—they add up to a harmonious, meaningful picture which is the setting of your dream. Food elements on a plate: meat, potatoes, a variety of diverse vegetables are all different but they add up to a balanced meal, or a full setting analogous to your dream. Symbols can be universally recognised—such as the elements of the cosmos or things that are given meaning through a story or scene. If you are familiar with the similies "Shall I compare thee to a summer's day?" (Sonnet 18, Shakespeare)—comparing one thing with another— and metaphors—one thing standing in place of another—"Thou art a summer's day," (not Shakespeare) you will understand the language that God uses to communicate with us. In *The Lion the Witch and the Wardrobe*, Aslan the lion is a symbol for Christ. The Bible is made up of narrative, poetry and prose. Approximately 43% of the Bible is made up of narrative, from historical narrative to parables and proverbs. Some 33% of the Bible is poetry, including lyrical language & song, reflective poetry, and the passionate, politically resistant and subversive poetic language of the prophets. The Bible teaches us that the Kingdom of God is like treasure that must be sought out. He does not throw his pearls before swine as illustrated by the biblical parables. The treasures of his communication are for those who are hungry for more of him—the bread of life—to search out. Some of us are hungrier than others. He also uses visual language because it is much more memorable. A picture paints a thousand words, as the saying goes. Words, unless they are uttered by Emily Dickinson, or Dylan Thomas, are not usually seized upon by the mind in the way that pictures or images are. God is a master painter. He paints the sky with sunsets and covers birds with clothes of many colours. Every colour is imbued with meaning. For example, blue is the colour of the heavens, and of revelation. Red is the colour of redemption, or love and passion, the colour of life, given life is in the blood and Jesus redeemed us from our sins. Symbolic language is the language of God. We are told through the Bible that when we are in eternity, we will communicate spirit to spirit, not through words though there is plenty of sound in heaven, not least the sound of singing and music! This visual language of God should become our *duo lingo pronto!* It is the language of our times and the last days language that the prophet Joel 2:28 in the Old Testament. Also later quoted by Paul in Acts 2:17.

Cultural Symbols

We all have symbols and idioms in the language of our culture. As you know, UK English abounds with Shakespearean phrases and idiomatic language: 'You are a rose among thorns...' 'all that glitters is not gold,' 'green-eyed monster,' 'wear my heart on my sleeve,' and 'break the ice' and so on. If you do not have these phrases the appearance of a rose in a bramble bush of thorns in a dream may mean something other than the phrase supplied in the second instance. If you saw a monster with green eyes in a dream, the 'green eyed monster,' synonymous with envy might spring to mind. An American friend recently used the word 'doozy' to describe a difficult dream to interpret. I'd never heard this in my life, given it's an American word. I shan't forget it though. All to show that God will use symbols and language references that he might bring to your mind in connection with an image or symbol in your dream. God will use symbols that are meaningful to you, but there are symbols such as wedding rings, cars, brides, houses and so on that are ubiquitous symbols.

Puns, riddles, idioms, Cockney Rhyming Slang and other word play

A crossword may be a 'cross' word. Or a cross (Jesus/word) and the Bible (word). I had a warning dream in which I was sitting with the English actor Michael York on a bench. There were grapes on the ground, not on the vine. In the dream Michael (I'm not saying the archangel Michael; though it would be cool if it was him!) was an angel or 'messenger' coming to warn me about an event that was about to take place near York, for which angelic assistance was needed. The grapes on the ground symbolised the danger of not being connected into Jesus the true vine, or remaining in the vine: "I am the vine, you are the branches," and I also heard the literary phrase 'Grapes of Wrath', the title of a William Faulkner novel, symbolising an upcoming situation that was threatening to flare up. The grapes on the ground (worldly) and not on the vine, highlighted a spiritual issue working through a number of people that the dream applied to. Apples & Pears may be stairs as they are in British Cockney Rhyming slang, a China plate might refer to a mate—friend; a loaf of bread a head and so on. Puns have a dual meaning. The sun could be a son and so on.

Phrases from books, songs and film and other languages

Is it ungodly that God might say "Beat it, just beat it," (Michael Jackson) in order for you to turn your face like flint from a situation that you are engaged with beyond God's timing or shouldn't be paying attention to? Or 'Play it again Sam,' for a reminder of something? No. I have loved pop music, film, photography, art and literature since I was a tiny child and learnt all the lyrics to songs that I later articulated with a hairbrush for a microphone on a veranda stage in Zimbabwe. Given I love music, literature and art, God often speaks to me through these media. ABBA could appear representing the father, Abba. When interpreting a dream, a song phrase will often come to mind to back up what I feel a symbol means. It is scripture, however that God gives me to back up the whole meaning of the dream. Don't be religious, but don't be misled either. God and the Bible are always the plumbline by which we measure the message. He does this in dreams, and he does this in waking life. There is a phrase from a novel *The Go-Between* (1953): "The past is a foreign country: they do things differently there." How we come to terms with our pasts, is something that all tend to work through to some extent. We are informed by the past, but we must evolve and change or we remain stagnant. If I don't rein myself in, I have a tendency to dwell on the past, but life must move on. If I am praying, and this is on topic, he might bring a phrase like this to me, through my mind during our conversation to trigger my awareness as to my state of mind. Similarly, if I am asleep and God is speaking to me he might speak through visual pictures that I appreciate, or are meaningful to me.

Symbols and Symbolic Language

When looking at general symbols ask your self a series of questions.
- Firstly, is it a positive or negative symbol? Grapes are often positive—fruit of the vine, wine, good for you. But as mentioned, and pertinent to me, there is also a Faulkner novel called *The Grapes of Wrath*. All symbols can have a positive or negative meaning in context. Where is the fruit? What is the state of the vine? Is the food up high or low down on the ground? Ripe or withered on the vine?
- Does it have a personal or cultural meaning?
- Is it biblical? Ravens fed the prophet Elijah after his encounter with Jezebel. They are bold, clever and playful—consider their characteristics. A lion can be the lion of Judah or the devourer, depending on context.
- If it's an object, what colour is it and what is it used for?
- Is it a dream symbol that you have seen before? Is God labouring a point that He wants to get through to you?
- Is God using word puzzles or puns or does He want you to mine for a deeper meaning such as with the Fiat car in my daughter's dream. Jot down a series

148

of possible meanings. The correct one will come to you as you go through all the symbols and see how they connect with each other. All the elements need to go together to build up the parable of the dream. Using the puzzle method helps—ask yourself, 'does this symbol make sense with that one, or that one?' More on this later. Soon a picture will emerge as you prayerfully consider each aspect of the dream.

Learn to decode poetry

Creativity, inspiration, and imagination are the wells that symbolic language arise from. One way to train your brain is to decode or at least take note of poetic or metaphorical (synonymous with symbolic) language. Study the resonant poetic language of the Bible. Begin to notice symbols in films, literature and most of all poetry. You can search for poems online at Poetry Foundation. Consider the skull in *Hamlet* as a symbol of death or the metaphorical phrase *All the world's a stage, And all the men and women merely players*: A comment on the fleeting nature of life and we the unwitting pawns on the stage going through the metamorphoses of life stages. *Shall I compare thee to a summer's day?* Here Shakespeare is comparing the object of his love to a summer's day. Get yourself a copy of poems or a clutch (a handy collective noun I made up) of Shakespeare sonnets. In a notebook decode all the metaphors that you find in your poem (akin to symbols) and note them down. One of my favourite poems is *Do Not Go Gentle into That Good Night* by the Welsh poet, Dylan Thomas. He uses metaphors of day and night as symbols for life and death. He uses the metaphoric phrase, 'do not go gentle into that good night' to mean 'fight against death.' He implores his father to literally rage against death: 'rage, rage against the dying of the light.' This poem is so spiritual and powerful! He pleads with his father to not accept death by telling him to "rage at the dying of the light." The 'dying of the light' as a phrasal metaphor for 'the end of the day' or death, when 'light' as a metaphor for life is extinguished. In William Blake's *The Tiger* (1774) the phrases "What immortal hand or eye," *the 'immortal hand or eye'* symbolises God's vision in creating the tiger and "Could frame thy fearful symmetry?" - speaks of the tiger itself as a metaphor of the incredibly ferocious creative force in human nature with potential for good or evil. Another poem rich with symbolism is *The Thought Fox* by the English poet, Ted Hughes, who often used animals as metaphors in his poetry. *The Thought Fox* is a poem about inspiration; being inspired to write poetry and the mysterious trigger that causes images to surface from the imagination in order to write a poem. In the poem, the fox is a metaphor for this process of 'sniffing out' a poem. (Not the poet's intention, but this is also useful metaphor for allowing the subconscious to give rise to dream symbols.) In the second stanza of the poem, the poet aptly shows a sense of something symbolic powerfully emerging as if through the darkness of the subconscious: "Through the window I see no star: something more near, though deeper within darkness is entering the loneliness." (TedHughes, Faber&Faber)

Decode the Psalms

God loves poetry which is why there is so much of it in the Bible. Take a Psalm a week and try to learn it by heart. Psalm 23 is a good one to start and one I know by heart, but you can take Psalm 1 and begin there. Be that tree with deep roots in the Holy Spirit. Take out your notebook or journal and write down the Psalm. Take every simile or metaphor (comparing one thing to another) and write it down. Studying the Proverbs will not only make you wise but more discerning when it comes to dream interpretation. Learning one a day is good practise. My children and I read them aloud together and then discuss how to apply them to everyday life.

Use your mind

Be mindful, there is a clear process of logic involved too. You can use your mind to reason! It is possible to become too religious over interpretation. God has given us a brain and thinking faculties for good reason—pardon the pun. We are supposed to use logic in building up a skillset to decode dreams. We use our brains and the Holy Spirit's revelation, it is as simple, and as difficult as that. God expects you to use your brain in a process of engagement. Begin one step at a time, just as if you were doing a crossword puzzle, word by word or symbol by symbol, and ask yourself, what does this mean in the Bible? What does this mean to me? Once you have asked this of all the symbols, or pictures—as in what does this noun—animal, place or thing—mean in my dream, look at the action of the dream. What is happening around the characters, symbols or elements of your dream? Who or what is the focus? What is the setting or the place of your dream? Is it a house? It often is—the house is you: your earthly body. The other people objects in the rooms or compartments of your life are aspects of yourself. If it is outside, why is there a vast open field—is it green? The field could be the world or be symbolic of new growth or beginnings. Is the field full of wheat? God may be asking you to go and reap a harvest, in which case, evangelism will be easy for you. Someone else has already done the sowing and God has done the growing! Use your wonderful brain. It is the hardware that God has given you and He expects you to use it and the more you do the more adept at interpretation you will become.

If a dream involves flying or soaring God could be elevating one to soar to greater spiritual heights. If they are in a long corridor the dreamer may be in a period of transition. If they are having their hair restyled, it may be in preparation for a new role. If a back door has been left open and an event from the past is coming back to the person, they may need to deal with unfinished business from the past. If dogs with bared teeth are at the gates of your town, God may be warning that the powers and principalities are getting ready to bring about their agenda. If there are spiders, there is witchcraft. Perhaps Jesus is knocking on a door and wants more access to your life. If there is a trapdoor, there is 'a trap' a door that the enemy is using for access. If this sounds confusing, you need to know that the setting of your dream and the context of it in your life is everything. Ask yourself, what does this symbol represent? Then look at the setting to see if the picture elements make sense in the bigger picture or setting. Apply this reasoning to other symbols such as other common symbols or features of dreams using symbology from everyday life, for example:

Natural Features—External Landscapes

A mountain could be symbolic of a person who looms large in your life or a 'high place' where you meet with God as Moses did 'on the mountain.' What do you do on a mountain? What did Moses do? Jesus? It's a place of His presence or encounter. It might be symbolic of effort or exertion. A tree could be a person as in Nebuchadnezzar's dream where he was identified by Daniel as a tree. Stars can be brothers. Context is all! The Holy Spirit can be the wind or the wind can represent change as in 'the winds of change.' Fire burns away chaff. Rivers can be the Holy

152

Spirit the river of His life or the cares of life threatening to overwhelm you. If it is muddy and rushing this could indicate a spiritual mix. The sea covers vast expanses of the earth and often signifies the tumult of the world—Psalm 98:7 "Let the sea resound, and all that fills it, the world, and all who dwell in it." Consider the nature of the terrain and landscape, and any seasonal or unusual features: Is that a face you see in that mountain?! Look at Bible verses that have mountains, rivers, wind, fire and so on in them.

Buildings and Rooms—Internal landscape

Given a house in a dream is usually you, the rooms are often aspects of your own life, like stage sets for different aspects of action that need to be attended to by you. Consider internal architecture or internal landscape—which can indicate features of your own heart. What colour is that sofa? A sofa is where you read your Bible or entertain friends - what do you do there? A bed is where you stop and rest for increments of time or a place of intimacy and deep communion. Consider the function of the room and what action is taking place there and why. Your 'why' is how it applies to the setting or meaning of the dream and the context of your life. A kitchen is where you cook up spiritual food; a basement is often to do with issues of the heart; the attic, the mind; a living room—a place where you entertain people—or thoughts and deeds; A bathroom is a place for cleansing and sometimes meditation - think of a bubble bath and candles—it depends on context and action. If you are on the toilet, there may be a need for deliverance or spiritual cleansing; a relaxing candlelit bath is one message, a bath with dirty water, another. Apply logic to the symbolism, then set them in the context of the bigger picture. A candle burning can symbolise the presence of the Holy Spirit. A church can be the presence of God. A castle can be the strong tower of the Lord or something scary and foreboding. An apartment block can represent the world as many people live there. A bridge can symbolise transition—moving from one place to another.

People

In dreams people can be angels or demons; trees; people representing other people, or aspects of yourself. Ask yourself who this person is to you or what they represent? They could represent the church or another organisation. How are they dressed? Are they wearing glasses or Wellington Boots—what do these details symbolise? An inability to see clearly? Feet protected from the weather of the world? Or are they prepared for their own Battle of Waterloo, as the Duke of Wellington was? What colour is their hair—have they just had it cut - if so they may be preparing for a change. If their hair is long they may be hiding behind it or trying to cover something up. If they are plaiting it they may be seeking to make a three stranded cord, or get closer to God—"Though one may be overpowered, two can defend themselves. A cord of three strands is not quickly broken." (Ecclesiastes 4:2). See what scriptures come to mind or do a Biblical word search. A bride often symbolises the people of God. A baby represents a new project or idea... or possibly the arrival of a new child if taken literally. A woman can represent the church, a husband Jesus or God the Father, or your actual father! What are the people in the dream doing? Ask yourself 'why?' Once, a fairly well known person who I hadn't yet met, came and kissed me on the cheek. The kiss signified that we would work together one day—it wasn't wishful thinking!

Animals

Animals can be aspects of your personality or other people's or countries and kingdoms—as in the case of Daniel's beasts. A sheep will be a follower—you/me/us—of Jesus or an animal that gives wool or meat. A pig can be unclean or not kosher; a policeman or a cute pet. Dogs can be demons, Jesus or a faithful friend. A dove is often the Holy Spirit or represents innocence; an eagle—America or a prophet. Snakes can be wise or liars or satan. Cows can be famines; foxes, liars, or people of wisdom or craftiness; a lion, the devourer but also Jesus.

Chapter 14. Prepare to Dream

The ability to remember dreams can depend on a variety of factors such as personality, creativity, mental state, cognitive functions as well as bodily symptoms, but there is much that we can do to help ourselves. It is very important that you sleep well. It is when we rest that we heal and rid ourselves of stress and anxiety. Too much alcohol and caffeine, interfere with sleep. In order to be a good conduit for dreams, ask God to sanctify your mind, so that you dream. You need to follow the Biblical mandate of being renewed in your mind. Learn scripture. God will reward you by using it to illustrate your dreams further. Read scripture aloud and listen to it daily. The Bible tells us that 'faith comes by hearing the word of God.' You need faith to hear from God. Sanctify your home with worship music. Tune out of ungodly guff on television or at the cinema or in movies. I know this doesn't leave much to watch, but make the choice to choose life. Read the classics instead. Or go for a walk. Be expectant and spiritually engaged—ready to receive your dream. The Bible tells us in Job that God delivers dreams every morning. 'Ask and you will receive.' Meditate on the Bible before bed, give thanks before bed. Try to go to bed at around the same time each night including on the weekends. Between 9:30pm and 11:30pm, seems to be a good time for most people. Ask God to wake you up to remember your dream. Have a pen handy to jot down dream elements or recorder ready I you must have electronic devices in your bedroom!) and then write it down and record it later.

Try to get 8 hours of sleep. For example, if you need to get up at 7am, you ideally want to be asleep at 11pm. But be prepared to make adjustments to this and don't get hung up on it which can wind you up, not down! For many, including *moi*, if I go to bed at 11pm, I might not fall asleep for at least an hour. Develop good habits. Try not to drink caffeine after midday—disclaimer. I find it really hard to follow my own advice on this one! Cut out late-night snacking— eating food close to bedtime messes with your digestion, which messes with your sleep and your dreams. Finish eating any food at least 2 to 3 hours before you want to fall asleep. Ban your phone from your *boudoir*. The blue light from phones and other electronic devices is known to overstimulate the mind. Although we know blue light is bad for sleep, but so is reading the news or any other emotion inducing content. Binge-worthy TV can make you too alert to sleep. Catch a Bible binge instead or listen to the dulcet tones of John Suchet reading through the audio Bible. Class. Turn off phone alerts. Switching off notification alerts and use night filters will help to minimise effects. Switch everything off at least 1 hour before bed. In fact, keeping electronic devices out of the bedroom altogether can be the best option for some people especially those of us that are peskily addicted. Develop a relaxing evening routine. Read, have a warm candle lit bath, listen to relaxing music/ worship music. Make your skincare routine a form of meditative practise. If you're struggling to switch off the thoughts going around your mind, try relaxation techniques. Keep a notebook by your bed to write down any lists or ideas or things you need to remember. Just jot things down and leave them. Making a to-do list for the next day can quiet your mind and improve your sleepiness and sleep quality. It's like clearing your mental desk to receive heavenly messages that you are not going to forget to write down!

Breathing Technique for Relaxation or Insomnia

4/7/8 Breathing
Start by sitting with your back straight.
Place the tip of your tongue on the tissue just behind your upper front teeth. Keep your tongue there throughout the exercise.
Breathe out through your mouth then close it.
Breathe in through your nose while counting to 4.
Hold your breath at the top of your lungs and count to 7.
Breathe out through your mouth and count to 8.
Repeat several times and practise daily if you feel anxious or stressed or need to relax.

Visualisation Exercise to Switch off a Busy Mind

Learn Psalm 23. As you go through it in your mind visualise each image in the Psalm. Take your time. As you lie in bed go through the Lord's prayer as you may have done that morning, but visualise your father in heaven and so on.

Prepare to Dream—The night Before

Thank God for all the accomplishments of the day. Repent or ask forgiveness for any ungodly thoughts or deeds. Ask God to sanctify the garden of your mind to dream and to meet with you there. Take several deep breaths in through your nose and out through your mouth: hold the inhale at the top of your lungs for a count of four and then exhale... and drift off to sleep. No counting sheep necessary unless they actually appear in your dream! Meditate on scripture before bed. When I go to bed at night I do so with thankfulness for everything that has been achieved in the day. I thank and praise God for the work he has done in my life that day and for our partnership in the spirit. I make sure I have my journal and pen ready to write down my dream according to Habakkuk 2:2, "Then the LORD replied: "Write down the revelation and make it plain on tablets so that a herald may run with it." Some record their dreams on voicemail, and this is fine in the first instance, but I find that when I begin to write out the dream, the revelation begins to come.

When you wake up

Before you reach for your journal—more on journaling soon—that is ready and waiting for you on your nightstand, press 'dream replay' and meditate on the dream before writing it down.

- Allow the scenes from the dream to float up from your subconscious. Replay it like a movie, taking careful note of each scene as you recall them. See it first in as much fullness as you can recall. Enlarge your dream in your memory—bring it up from your subconscious before you even get out of bed or engage in any other activity or even *think* about coffee.
- Then do an initial recording by jotting it down, and allow free association—the method of allowing your mind to 'float' in an uncensored way. You can make further sense of things as you go along.
- I often speak it out loud to family first, which helps me to not only recall further, but to begin the process of interpretation. As I am speaking the Holy Spirit begins to impart meaning—I then pick up my journal and begin decoding the dream..
- I date it and give it a title: "Swan Eating Fish Dream" or "Fighter Jets over Wales," etc.
- Then write it out in draft form using the methods I will show you. Sometimes I use a combination of

the arrow method (I explain what this is later on) and doodling or drawing.

- As I write, the Holy Spirit, who 'brings all things to remembrance,' will usually give me the meaning of the symbols in the dream as well as the dream's setting—if a sofa appears in my dream, as well as a bed in another scene of the dream, and me sitting on a beach in a third scene in the dream, along with the number 7, I will understand that God is asking me to take a break, or is instructing me on the importance of rest. If I am being hasty—running and tripping over, say—in my dream, he may well be telling me to be patient. If twins appear along with the number 14, I know I am in for a double blessing, which is a wonderful double whammy!

- There may well be successive drafts of the dream necessary as you mine for revelation, particularly with national/international dreams.

- If you don't feel you have the whole meaning more or less, straight away, pray in the spirit, which helps you connect more deeply with the spirit of God, and try again.

- Write another draft and use another method (from the interpretation toolkit section) to trigger meaning.

- If more revelation is needed, mull on it for the rest of the day. In my experience, as you are faithful in recall and documentation, God will be faithful in bringing the fullness of meaning. He will 'trouble' you with it until you engage with Him for full interpretation.

- If you are faithful, He will rise to His faithfulness, and the meaning will come one way or another— through Him or you, as you pray and meditate on it over hours, days or even weeks, or through an interpreter. If the meaning still does not come document it anyway, in case revelation comes later or God adds meaning through another dream. Sometimes God speaks over a series of dreams.

Free Association

When you are interpreting with God allow your brain to 'free associate' in the first instance. Allow ideas and thoughts and symbols to bubble up from your subconscious without censoring them. Scribble down all possibilities with question marks—don't judge or dismiss. Human beings have a tendency to judge or dismiss ideas as 'coming from them' or as too daft or whako for consideration. Don't! This is an order. Your Holy Spirit saturated mind (you have prayed/prayed in the spirit first!) can sort through the symbol ideas later. God is adept at making order out of chaos, so trust the process. You will get to the big bang of truth (see what I did there?) before long. Be patient yet determined. Consider this a 'first draft' of dream interpretation or a first attempt or analysis. Once you have done this over the whole dream, you can go back over it a second time (the second draft) and allow your mind to apply reasoning and logic to all the elements and symbols of the dream. Successive drafts may be needed as revelation comes. I will show you how I do this later.

Warning Light: Electronic Devices

If you wake in the night, you can record your dream into your phones voice recorder to note it down (assuming you haven't removed the devices from your room!) Or scribble it down on some paper you keep next to your bed, but do not miss out the vital step of faithfully writing the dream down. In the act of writing, God often quickens the meaning there and then, or even gives you more revelation. It is in the act of writing the dream down that God often gives me a scripture or verse from the Bible to illuminate the dream further or to confirm it.

Dream Snatches and Dream Snatchers

When I was a child in Zimbabwe I used to catch the
big coloured butterflies that flitted above the flowers
in our garden like tiny kites or birds. There would be
a flash of wing and then they would disappear only to
reappear again a moment later, elsewhere. Often you
will awake from a dream and not be able to
remember it. Quickly record the images that have
flashed from your subconscious to your conscious
mind like the turns of a kaleidoscope. If God has
something to say He will reveal it. If nothing else, it is
good to record every detail in case more is revealed at
a later date, in days to come, or perhaps by a feeling
of *de ja vu t*hat will trigger a recollection that is
revealed by the former image in a previous dream.
These dream snatches are more like photographic
images than film images but they should not be
dismissed as, if from God, they can be quickened to
the mind in due course, and God can give revelation
to us from them as we meditate on them. In Micah
1:1, we learn that the prophet Micah saw the word of
the Lord: "The word of the LORD that came to Micah
of Moresheth during the reigns of Jotham, Ahaz and
Hezekiah, kings of Judah—the vision he *saw*
concerning Samaria and Jerusalem." As we lie in bed
on waking we need to see these images afresh as we
recall them and then record them in our journals, not
dismiss them because they may not be sequential. As
we faithfully record, God may give us *rhema*
revelation as we record, or we file them away in our
journals for potential further use or recollection—
they are there for us to literally *re*collect again.

Journaling

"In the first year of Belshazzar king of Babylon, Daniel
had a dream, and visions passed through his mind as

he was lying in bed. He wrote down the *substance* of
his dream."
Daniel 7:1

It is very important to keep a journal and to write
down every dream. Writing by hand uses a different
brain pathway than typing on a keyboard. A new
study has investigated neural networks in the brain
during hand- and typewriting. "The researchers
showed that connectivity between different brain
regions is more elaborate when letters are formed by
hand. This improved brain connectivity, which is
crucial to memory building and information
encoding, may indicate that writing by hand supports
learning,"[10]. I always handwrite but have begun to
later type and file them on a computer as I have
stacks of journals. The old school method of
handwriting should not be discarded however, as it
stimulates the brain to recall and boosts creativity. It
is also more calming and meditative. Not like bashing
away on keys! In order to decode your dreams you
will need a notebook and a pen and a bible that you
keep by your bed. *Fin!* The reason you record your
dreams is so that you can note when a foretelling
dream comes to pass, but also so that you can learn
the language of your own dreams in order to decode
them. The dream is locked up, but you will be given
the decoding key if you are patient. You need to learn
which way to turn the key to unlock the door to the
heavenly realm from where your dream came from.
The meaning, or the gist of the meaning will likely
emerge fairly quickly, as with the process of putting a
negative image into photographic solution and
hanging the developing image up. This process of
development comes as the picture is exposed to the

---

[10] https://www.frontiersin.org/news/2024/01/26/writing-by-
hand-increase-brain-connectivity-typing

light and the 'solution' of the Holy Spirit. However, some dreams require prayer and meditation. I call this 'mulling over the dream.' This can be hours or sometimes weeks. I note down any further revelation in my dream journal and sometimes add sticky notes and drawings later. Daniel sometimes took two weeks over a dream. As with Daniel's high level dreams, an angel was required to bring revelation—usually Gabriel, though the archangel Michael put in an appearance too. This shows us that there can be interference from the second realm between God's revelation coming and your receiving it. Given that most dreams are personal, this may not happen, but not out of the question. At any rate, if you are faithful with your dreams, God will be faithful to supply the meaning as you write them down and meditate over them. It is imperative that you write the vision or dream down. As you do so, the Holy Spirit will begin to quicken revelation to you, and scripture will likely come to mind to back it up. After I have written down the dream, I ask the revealer of mysteries, to reveal the dream to me as Daniel did. I then begin to decode the symbols of the dream. Diarise all your visions and prophecies too. Otherwise how can you prove to yourselves and others if need be, when they come to pass? "Then the LORD replied: "Write down the revelation and make it plain on tablets so that a herald may run with it." (Habbakuk 2:2).

Chapter 15. Decoding

Most dreams require decoding, unless they play out like scenes in a movie that need little interpretation. The code of the dream, is the sequence that unlocks your dream as revealed by the symbols in most dreams. These are literal dreams. Sometimes they have scenes, like scenes in a play or in a movie. Often there will be three or four scenes based on a theme. A theme is the central message that God is trying to convey. For example, the central message of a play or film, might be that good conquers evil, or that education is the key to understanding, or, that you don't need to be high born to aim high and conquer the heights. The plot or the scenes in the dream are the vehicles of the message, and the symbols are the carriers of the message, the code that points up or illuminates the message. They are like lightbulbs, lighting up meaning.

Be a Detective as you decode

As you begin to decode the symbology of your dream, ask yourself questions about each symbol within the setting of your dream. Here are some example questions with possible answers. Again, note these will be different according to the setting of your dream.
- Is that my husband? It is Jesus who can appear as my husband.
- Why is Mildred wearing that ghastly frock with giant strawberries on? She is about to have a fruitful summer.
- Why is this dog running round in circles chasing it's tail? The dog could be a person who keeps making the same mistakes over and over again—this is an

English expression for getting nowhere: a dog chasing its tail, "like a dog returning to its vomit"— you could find out that last bit by looking up what dogs represent in the Bible.

- Why is that pastor over pumped with muscles like a superhero? He's doing things in his own strength.
- Why am I talking to those air hostesses? They are ministering angels sent to help you
- Why are they in that overland vehicle? They are being sent on a dangerous clandestine mission in the spirit/or actual mission
- Why is that woman bringing up the bones of her dead husband? She is still grieving and God wants to release her from her lingering negative emotional attachments in order for her to move on in life.
- Why is that penguin in my pool and in the sea? The penguin is a person who is called to the church (pool) as well as the sea (world) they are at home in or called to a variety of settings for the work they are to do—possibly evangelism. (Penguins are at home on land, sea and even pools!).

Decoding Lists

The simplest way to decode is to write your dream out, then underline the symbolism or use a highlighter pen. Then list the symbols, decode them and apply the message to the setting of the dream and the context of your life but I will show you some of the many creative ways you can help yourself arrive at the message of the dream later in this book. You can use coloured pens for various symbols if you want to get creative. Look at your list of symbols taken from your dream. See if you can discern what each symbol means. Remember one symbol will stand for another. In the UK we have nativity calendars where children open one secret window per day of the month. Behind the window is a little toy or chocolate shape. Behind each symbol of your dream lies a hidden meaning, depending on the context of the dream or its intrinsic or subjective meaning to you. A fish might mean a Christian; a dragon, satan; an apple health or temptation; it might imply knowledge as in Eve's apple, you can only tell what is going on when the symbols start to resonate and the clues begin to add up to a full picture. It all depends on your own symbology and the context of the dream. Remember to ask yourself, and God, questions, such as who does this person, animal or thing represent? Once you have a list of symbols apply them to the setting. They are the clues that unlock the secret message of the dream.

Setting

Imagine a garden with a flowerbed full of a variety of beautiful designed and patterned flowers. Each flower will be imbued with a specific meaning, but the soil in which these symbols 'grow' is the bed from which the meaning is embedded. The 'garden' or setting of your dream is very important. Your symbols will be embedded in soil—symbolic of your heart—and planted with other symbols that resonate with each other, or illuminate one another. The setting will be harmonious; the symbols are like instruments, with each playing their part to produce the melody, or message of the dream. If one symbol is not heard the harmony will be discordant. Each symbol has meaning and will be placed in the ideal setting for the meaning of that dream to come forth. A vehicle may appear on a road or off the road, indicating a problem or something that needs to be attended to. If you are driving that vehicle the vehicle is your means of travel for work or ministry and the road is your life. The road may go up in the direction of mountains, it is on the mountain that Moses met God face to face, so your driving towards the mountains means that there is an invitation to you to go higher to meet with the Lord on His holy mountain. Is it night? If so, your dream could have a dark connotation or warning. Is it bright daylight? Are people happy? This is another connotation entirely. This is why setting and situation is important to understand, as is atmosphere, and emotion—how you feel in the dream—are you happy or sad? Is your dream dark or light? Did you feel at home or displaced? Is it light or dark? Day or night? Everything is meaningful in a dream. All of these factors have a bearing on the meaning of a dream. You need to build up a full picture. It's like a puzzle. All the pieces matter. If one piece is missing you will not get a complete picture. Remember those Fuzzy Felt pictures, readers of a certain age? You had to apply the objects and animals and people to the city house or field for it all to build up a picture or story. If a link in the chain is missing, the necklace will fall apart and all those pearls of wisdom will bounce around the floor! As you write down your dreams, the symbols will reveal themselves to you. Each symbol is a part of the picture—and the picture is the fulfilment of the dream or the message that God is giving the dreamer that needs to be applied to the context of your life what you are going through when you had the dream, or what your heart preoccupations were, or what the answers you were looking for from God are.

Big Picture, Small Picture

Imagine your mind's eye as a big camera. Focus on the main action of the dream, or the big picture. Where is the central action taking place? Who is the action taking place around? In other words, what is the focus of the dream? Who is the action affecting?

Most likely you, if you are in the dream in any way shape or form which you usually are. You may be in camera or off camera. Then begin to move your camera around. Who or what else is in the dream? Are there other people? What do they mean? Remember other people can be other people—a farmer could be Jesus or the pharisees, or a farmer! You will need to apply everything to the context of your own life to get the interpretation. What else is in the dream? What is the internal or external landscape or terrain like? Bring your focus in now and look at the details. Perhaps there is furniture in the room if it takes place in an internal setting. Are there doors and windows? Are they open or closed? Curtains? Blinds? Colours? Numbers? Everything is significant. My daughter had a dream of a friend sitting amongst pigs on a farm. Why was she outside without boundaries? She was on her phone. Therefore my daughter knew she had to pray for her friend and what she was watching and receiving on her phone. Pigs are unclean animals in the Bible and there was resonance with the parable of the prodigal son, as such it was a warning dream. My daughter prayed about it and acted on the dream sensitively.

Context

A dream has no meaning unless it is applied to the circumstances of your own life. It is important to write a title to your dream and the date. If you can provide a context for the dream—ie. what is happening in your own life at the time, then you can embed the dream in context or keep the context in mind if more messages from God on that theme arrive in subsequent dreams, which again, you note down in similar fashion with dates, titles and the substance of the dream decoded and embedded in context. A dream is like a plant that cannot flourish unless it is sprung from the soil of your circumstances. Once you have decoded your dream, place it in context, in other words, apply it to your life. Is your daughter having a difficult time at school? Are the symbols in your dream indicative of answers to a question you have been praying about in connection with your daughter? Did a man or woman appear in your dream and put their arm around your child? If so, there is no need for you to worry, God is showing you that their guardian angel is protecting them. Most of your dreams will be about you and your life circumstances.

Application or Action

God sends you heavenly messages with a purpose. When you have decoded your dream or understood your night vision, ask God, What is the purpose of this dream? How do I apply it to my own life? Sometimes this will be obvious. My husband often has very simple direct dreams. He jokes that God makes things simple for him. Mine often require more study and decoding, and they are not always about me. My daughter has very specific dreams in terms of timing. She has that Issachar anointing! My second son had a dream in which he and I were taken to the court of Solomon. The dream revealed that my son who had turned twelve and was thus coming into a new phase of spiritual maturity and 'growing in wisdom and stature,' was to be taught the ways of wisdom. This intellectual child is unusually wise for his years—he is the one who saw the lions—but what he was seeing was a picture of himself sitting in the counsel of the wise—the Holy Spirit as typified by Solomon. It was an invitation to the courts of the king to study with Him. I, as his mother or guide in the dream have the role of leading him there, as I have been training him and all my children in the ways of the kingdom of

God, not least in the area of wisdom that dream interpretation requires. His dream shifted to a scene where he was preparing for battle. This scene or aspect of the dream revealed a further training module if you like, given our battle is not against flesh and blood. When the dream came my son and I were just coming to the end of our season of reading the Psalms every evening, and were about to begin studying the Proverbs. This was the context of the dream and how it needed to be applied to our lives. God was encouraging both of us as in the way we should go. Sometimes the requirement of the dream will be to intercede. If God gives you a dream where you see what is happening in the dark realms, you need to act to pray or intercede. Someone came to me recently with a dream that seemed like a nightmare. But once decoded the dream showed a satanic agenda whereby the dreamer saw how satan had played his hand. There was a request to intercede and frustrate, or nullify the plans of the enemy. Sometimes you will be required to act on your dream if it concerns other people. National or international events are usually shared to intercede for, or to frustrate satanic agendas.

Dream Scenes and Sequences

You will find that as you dream, your dreams usually unfold in scenes or sequences. I number each scene of the dream or write them in sections on the page. Sometimes it will feel like you've had a number of dreams in a night but really they are scenes along a theme—they have a similar meaning that adds up to the message of the dream—like Josephs sheaves and stars. Different scenes, same meaning or message.

Dream Themes—The Hidden Message

In a book or movie, the action unfolds in a series of scenes, just like the scenes that make up the chapters of a book that the writer wants you to visualise. The scenes that make up the movie carry the theme, or the hidden message in the movie or book that the writer wants you to grasp. For example, in my first book, After the Rains (Emily Barroso), the question at the heart of the novel is Who owns the land? Another question was, can you ever forgive a friend who has participated in the politically motivated murder of a family member? I 'illustrated' or drew out the meaning of these themes with scenes that pointed up the meaning at the heart of the book, the messages that I wanted the reader to grasp and ponder. I did this by 'showing, not telling.' Telling or exposition is a cardinal sin in literature and can lead to excommunication from the canon of literature—just kidding, but you get the point. Similarly, your dream will often unfold in shifting scenes. The scenes will have different unfolding action but if it is from God it will make intelligible sense, God is trying to show you something that makes sense to you in your waking life. Each scene will carry the theme of the dream— try saying that multiple times over and over! If the theme does not carry through logically it may not be from God, but write it down and extract any meaning you can and note it down. It may be helpful later.

Emotions

Pay attention to how you feel in dreams. Do you feel anxious or joyful? Are you upset or troubled? Emotions have a bearing on the interpretation. How did you feel when you woke up from the dream? Go to God for prayer and reassurance and to help you direct your emotions appropriately. He is our counsellor.

Dreams from God are compelling. Consider how the baker and cup bearer felt after their dreams, or Nebuchadnezzar's turmoil after he's had the dream he could not remember. Always record how you felt in the dream and how you feel when you wake up. This will help you to contextualise your dream.

Colours

As we boarded the London bus we took to school one day. my eldest, visionary son, told me that the colour red made him feel uncomfortable—I can't remember the exact word, and he may have been equating the colour with his school uniform, and the constriction this bright creative child felt in the confines of school, but he was describing a strong, visceral reaction. (Red is the colour of viscera as well as passion and the blood of Jesus) Colours have a powerful effect on our emotions and along with numbers, are deeply meaningful. Blue, a heavenly colour, is the colour of revelation, brown is of the earth and nature or the dust from which we came; yellow is a hopeful colour but it can also signify cowardice. Green can mean new life, wisdom or envy. Purple is synonymous with royalty but can also indicate pride. You can do a Bible search on all the colours and numbers online, but make sure you apply them according to context and not verbatim. Ask the Holy Spirit for discernment.

Chapter 16. Mining for Revelation: National and International Dreams

Remember that photograph analogy I gave you for the process of dream interpretation? Sometimes a number of analyses or iterations of the dream interpretation over a period of days and weeks are required until a dream's hidden message fully emerges. Particularly with national or international dreams. I call this process mining for revelation: going in deep to seek out the symbolic jewels buried in the dream. Daniel was greatly affected by his dreams of the beasts he saw in Daniel 7&8, he did not always initially fully comprehend the full meaning of the dream. "This is the end of the matter. I, Daniel, was deeply troubled by my thoughts, and my face turned pale, but I kept the matter to myself." (Daniel 7:28). In Daniel 8, Gabriel was sent to help Daniel with the interpretation. "I was astonished by the vision, but no one understood it." (Daniel 8:27). Part of the vision of Daniel 8 has been fulfilled. However Daniel was told to "seal up the vision, for it refers to many days in the future." (Daniel 8:26). He was told to do the same concerning the vision of The Great Tribulation, the 'time of the end' (Daniel 12:9) that Jesus refers to in Matthew 24:15; in which he quotes Daniel. Daniel would not have had clarity on his dreams and visions were it not for angelic intervention and direct discussions with God in his dreams.

According to the patterns laid down in scripture, we can expect these events to be fulfilled in due course. On that note, it is helpful to remember that the Bible is a book of prophecy with predictions coming to pass: the circumstances of the birth, death and resurrection of Jesus for example; the captivity of the Jews and so on. I encourage you to study this for yourself. You can begin by simply googling it. The site, Got Questions[11] is quite helpful in this regard. Suffice to say that the Bible is a book of prophecies that have come to pass and the history of God's people, both the Jewish people and the Gentiles (us: those adopted into His family), moves through time and is engaged with, and is part of, actual, documented events of history. The Bible is not a 'make it up as you go along book,' but a book of actual history, with actual historical events and prophecies that were witnessed to and came and are coming to pass. Thus, we can expect the prophetic vision of Revelation to come to pass, along with other prophecies as yet to be fulfilled, as is the case of Daniel's visions that predict the rise and falls of empires: the empire of the Medes and Persia; Alexander the Great; the Roman Empire and so on. The book of Daniel is the book that I have found most helpful in working out international events. I encourage you to study both Daniel 7 and Daniel 8 and the outworking of these dreams in history. When one receives an international dream, the working out of it can be complex and may require multiple bouts of analysis, as further revelation or a new depths of meaning comes. This sometimes depends on how much time you have to give to the dream, and I confess that when this one came I was so busy with this book and other business that I did not decode beyond draft two until the recent conflict between Israel and Iran (on 13th April 2024), which acted as a wake up call to begin the mining process of the dream; but also, the revelation is dependent on God enlightening us and sometimes this happens in

---

[11] www.gotquestions.org/

due course given interference or contention for the revelation as indicated by the battles in the realms that delayed the angel getting to Daniel. I want to make it clear that this 'mining for deeper revelation' does not change the meaning of the dream. There is only one message, sealed or otherwise but sometimes, getting to that full meaning is deep work. In the case of this dream it took me 5 weeks to fully comprehend the interpretation of the dream. Incidentally, 5 is the number of God's grace, and I needed a lot of it with this dream.

I had the dream on the 4th April 2024. I was away so wrote the first draft interpretation in note format in my notes app on my phone. A second draft was written by hand, to document the dream, then a third which I sent out for prayer on WhatsApp. Then a fourth, fifth, sixth and seventh draft as the message continued to 'speak,' or reveal itself as it were and finally a piece of literature summed it up. By way of example, I am publishing this process so that you can see how I engage with mining for deeper revelation to access the full interpretation of the dream.

Before you read the dream, I would like to make something clear. God loves all nations, and even when leaders of nations act corruptly, or appear to act in an unseemly manner, Jesus is very concerned for the peoples of those nations. There are new alliances and agendas, religious, political, nationalistic and otherwise being plotted and formed in the earth now. These can be seen as 'empires.' There was once a vast and dominant British Empire and America too can be seen as an empire, given its economic influence and the power of the dollar, so we mustn't be too quick to judge, given the backyards of our own nations can be littered with rubbish as it were. History shows us that kingdoms rise and fall. God sets leaders of nations in place and can pull them down according to His purposes, as aptly illustrated by Nebuchadnezzar and the Babylonian empire. Our role is to pray for wisdom and strategy in the outworking of national and international dreams and always to pray for any potential disaster to be averted as God leads us. As the people of God we can be confident that as the days grow darker, God will shine brighter through us for the greater works as we align ourselves with His purposes. We must not forget that Daniel was a captive in Babylon when he interpreted dreams and visions for despotic kings and had his own dreams and visions of the great empires of history rising and falling, and saw what was to come at the end of the age. God worked in and through all these empires and the epochs of history and He still does. It's not helpful to swallow political rhetoric or propaganda wholesale along the lines of our nations being the 'goodies' and other nations 'baddies' though like Daniel we worship our God unflinchingly and with absolute dedication. Daniel was very respectful of the kings he was in service to however wicked they are seen to be. We have to try to be objective when seeking God for the interpretation for these dreams; if we wear our subjective glasses we could end up subverting the message according to our own intellect or biases which contravenes scripture: Trust in the LORD with all your heart and lean not on your own understanding; in all your ways submit to him, and he will make your paths straight, (9 Proverbs 3:5-6). We must be patient and prayerfully wait for the message to emerge, sometimes from deep waters. We should still call good, good and evil, evil—this form of absolutism is imperative, but none other. As with personal and other types of dreams, we need to put an international dream in context, which can require more extensive research and prayer, particularly if our knowledge of current affairs is less *au courant* than we might hope for it to be, but we must also be careful to try not to 'frame' the dream (in both senses) around our research. I find that if the interpretation has not fully arisen, I will continue to feel 'troubled' by the dream.

"There will be signs in the sun, moon and stars. On the earth, nations will be in anguish and perplexity at the roaring and tossing of the sea." Luke 21:25

2nd Draft: The Dream as it came before interpretation:

A Dream of Three Beasts: *Chinese Leopard Snake; Persian Leopard and Large Black Bear*
I dreamt of a large official looking lawn with very clipped and well attended green grass, like the ones in front of government buildings. I glimpsed white government buildings through the gates. At the far end of the lawn was a wild, bushy wilderness area. At the edge of the grass, between the lawn and the wilderness area, I saw the arms and hands of several people placing a large pregnant snake with leopard print markings. Not markings I am familiar with. Next a leopard was placed there in the same fashion. Again this leopard was a different shape to leopards I am familiar with. In fact the pregnant forms of both beasts were similar in shape. Then a large black bear and a woman appeared on the lawn dressed in a pale blue skirt and white top. Her yellowy hair appeared to be dyed blonde. The bear ran around on the lawn with the woman. She seemed to be some kind of trainer or had some kind of interaction with or influence over the bear that was running around hectically with her. It was as though they were tracking each other. The dream shifted and the bear was now swimming in the swirling sea that was in a globe shape: as if I saw it from the vantage point of space. The sea was tumultuous across the part of the globe that I could see. The woman swam underneath the bear. A long

thick black block, the length of a short pole but black and geometrical, divided them as they swam. Then the Bear was at the gates, I glimpsed white buildings through the gates—like the White House gates, where he turned into a man in a black suit.

Later that night, I dreamt I was with a Chinese child near a door in an open doorway. I was helping the child to walk. Later I was near a bed helping this child learn to read.

Primary elements in the dream:

The three beasts—Bear, Leopard and Leopard Snake —the last 2 were pregnant and were placed there by several arms and hands

A blonde woman dressed in blue and white.

A man who came from the bear

A sea (spherical in nature) in which the bear and the woman swam between a black block border

An area of overgrown bush

An area of carefully manicured lawn

Black gates behind which stood white buildings (akin to or actually the White House)

A black, geometric shaped, non organic block between the woman and the bear

3rd Draft Interpretation

Soon after I had this dream, Iran launched an attack on Israel on 13th April 2024. This provided me with a context into the interpretation of the dream. Due to the urgency of the situation I quickly wrote a brief interpretation and sent it out to some trusted believers to pray. The interpretation was as follows:

The dream was a warning of an alliance between three nations: Russia (the bear), Iran (the leopard) and China (the leopard snake). I had to look up these latter two animals in order to decode what nations they represented. The leopard was not a lean, slim, lithe African leopard that I knew of from being a Zimbabwean. It was different in shape, like the rare Persian leopard. The snake had leopard spots, akin to the Persian leopard, and it was shorter than most snakes I knew from Africa—only about a metre long. After researching online I found it was a leopard snake—a creature I hadn't even heard of—and one that is found in China. I felt the woman was an 'enemy agent' and the bear turning into a man represented the Antichrist at the gates of white government buildings like we see in the west (the White House). The pregnant beasts are pregnant with evil intent. The bushy overgrown area represented a world of chaos and demonic agenda. The churning sea was symbolic of tumult in the world and the bear was operating in the rising of the seas. As I sought revelation from God I was pointed to Indonesia and this gave further insight later on.

In the Bible the sea is a metaphor for chaos and symbolic of the nations of the earth. "Listen! The armies of many nations roar like the roaring of the sea. Hear the thunder of the mighty forces as they rush forward like thundering waves." (Isaiah 17:12 NLT) "Therefore thus saith the Lord God; Behold, I am against thee, O Tyrus, and will cause many nations to come up against thee, as the sea causeth his waves to come up, (Ezekiel 4:3 NKJ). However, I was reminded that God is in control and sets boundaries: "Do you not fear me? declares the Lord. Do you not tremble before me I placed the sand as the boundary for the sea, a perpetual barrier that it cannot pass; though the waves toss, they cannot prevail; though they roar, they cannot pass over it. (Jeremiah 5:22 ESV)

4th Draft Interpretation

God then made it clear to me that I did not yet have the revelation of the dream though I was 'on track.' As I sought the Lord further, I did more research into the elements of the dream—the animals and their characteristics and the arms and hands that placed the animals. I also heard "From Russia With Love, From Russia with love, I fly to you." The storyline of the original book by Ian Fleming was about a Communist Bloc assassination plot and was changed in the film to tone down the Cold War politics. Now there is a new world order that has formed: between Russia, China and Iran. Given the snake and the leopard had similar markings I knew there was an importance to the alliance of Iran and China— perhaps representative of their weapons: the 'arms' that placed them at the boundary of chaos (the wild area) and order (the lawn). Russia and China have historically supplied weapons and parts to Iran. Russia has been using Iranian drones to attack Ukraine. Iran is now an exporter of arms and drones. As I mentioned in draft 3, God had pointed me to Indonesia (also a mostly Islamic nation) and after researching I came upon a website that reported Indonesia's deep concern over the conflict arising between Iran and Israel and calling for restraint. Indonesia's Foreign Ministry urged the United Nations Security Council to respond to the rise in conflict to prevent further escalation in the Middle East[12]. I also read on Monday, April 15th, 2024 that Indonesia's economic minister, Mr Hartarto was taking steps to maintain market confidence amidst potential disruptions in commodity supplies, especially oil, and consequent increases in gold prices

---

[12] https://en.antaranews.com/news/310782/indonesia-calls-for-restraint-following-irans-attack-on-israel)

and to reduce the risk to the flow of goods in the Suez Canal, affecting cargo costs and supplies such as wheat, oil, and production components from Europe. All of which may answer the question as to why Indonesia as an actor in association with the dream came to mind. I had no idea they (Indonesia) were such a key player, and have been able to pray for wisdom regarding Indonesia and their role in de-escalating the conflict given it's potential impact on the world economy not least the supply of goods in the Suez Canal.

It is wise to take these dreams to those with whom you are in good counsel with for their wisdom and input as well. When I took this dream to one in my circle whom I trust, he saw that the wilderness/wild bushy area was also symbolic of a hiding place (a dense area of vegetation that was chaotic); but now the creatures were being brought out into the open, ordered clipped governmental lawns: onto the world government stage. The wilderness symbolises the demonic principalities that influence nations: the seat of demonic agendas. He also wondered if the blonde woman in the dream could be Europa (Europe) or the UN. She was wearing blue—the colour of Europe, but the yellow colour of her hair and the particular blue of her skirt are present in the Ukrainian flag and after a study of the colours of the woman's hair and clothing, this is what made sense to me. Heed the warning here. *This made sense to me* at the time, but it was not to be the final interpretation and I remained 'troubled' as to the symbolism of the woman. We only see in part or what God shows us and good counsel can come and cover our 'blind spots,' but also these conversations sharpen our own spiritual discernment and God is in them. But do only take your dreams to wise counsellors that you know well and who have the gift of wisdom, or confusion can arise confusion is not of God.

5th Draft interpretation

After God prompted me, about what He referred to as an 'unholy trinity,' I had further revelation and confirmation on the dream after studying Daniel 7&8, which encouraged me that I was on the right track in terms of the beasts representing empires—current 'empires,' being formed in the turmoil of the nations of the sea: symbolic of the world. Daniel's four beasts in Daniel 7 rose up out of the sea (symbolic of the nations of the world). I was also reminded that in 2013, God had warned me of an alliance between Islam and China. In previous drafts, I needed to discern who the woman was exactly, but after sharpening myself with wise counsel and further prayer, I understood she was not only Ukraine, but also Europe. *I understood* the meaning of the 'block' as a border: previously Ukraine was part of the communist 'bloc' and the border between Ukraine and Russia is disputed. I italicise this as I was speculating here or 'leaning on my own understanding': this was not the final revelation about the block. (It is okay to free associate at first. Sometimes the surface of your understanding needs to be 'skimmed off' like scum on simmering stew say, so that the rich meat beneath can be perceived.) The grass is symbolic of the ordered governmental world of western governments given it was in front of white buildings like Whitehall or the White House, in orderly form as apposed to the demonic chaos of the bushy area. When I googled images of the White House, the gates and lawn were the same. The leopard and the snake had been placed by human hands into this ordered space. The bear invaded the grassy lawn and ran amok with the woman in white and blue tracking it—following it.

Given I'd heard 'the enemy is at the gates,' I felt the man who came from the bear (Russia) at the gates was the Antichrist in some form, possibly Islam. I pondered whether he got there because of strategic alignments between Russia and the other two countries, fuelled by the war in Ukraine. Sasha Lensky writing in The Spectator (17th March 2024) noted that in 2019, the chief Mufti Ravil Gainutdin predicted that, by 2030, a third of Russia would be Muslim. Ms Lensky points out that Russia needs Chechen fighters to feed the Ukraine war and the trade off for Putin might be the Koran being taught in schools rather than Dostoyevsky (who incidentally was a Christian). I'd like to make it clear that this is not an attack on Muslims, whom God loves as people, but the spirit of a religion that the Bible would not recognise and is contrary to Christ's teachings, and that denies that Christ is God and is therefore 'antichrist.' The religion of Islam sees Jesus as a prophet and respects him as such but categorically does not see him as the Christ. There are other religions founded by lone prophets in caves that I don't agree with either, but I respect the sincere people of all faiths, and honour their right to think and choose as they see fit, and one hopes for reciprocity. At any rate, Islam is spreading rapidly and believers need to wake up to this 'enemy at the gates' that proliferates through war and destruction and makes war against the people of God.

I was also reminded that the three beasts signify countries with borders being disputed and land contended for, like Daniel's beasts signified kingdoms. "The four great beasts are four kings that will rise from the earth," (Daniel 17). Iran, Russia and China are not kingdoms, though they once were. These countries are not happy about American dominance on the world stage. Nevertheless, they are countries with autocratic rulers who want to increase their land and take over countries: look at China/Taiwan and Russia/Ukraine. Iran wants to dominate the Middle East. I read this op-ed by Hal Brands at The

American Enterprise Institute, a public policy think tank: *The ghosts of empire are haunting Eurasia. President Xi Jinping's China is seeking to reclaim the power and privileges of the great dynasties that once bestrode Asia. President Vladimir Putin is channeling the memory, and the methods, of famous conquerors from Russia's imperial past. Iran is using proxies, missiles and other means to build a sphere of influence encompassing parts of the old Persian Empire. Not so long ago, much of the world was ruled by empires. If today's revisionist states have their way, the future could resemble the past.*

Another key piece of the revelation concerned the pregnant beasts. What are they pregnant with? The next generation or the next phase of the world stage. What will the world look like in 20 years if we don't pray? What will the next generation birth? The Islamic world domination that Iran is determined to establish along with other islamic nations and groups is incubating as we speak. *The mullahs (of Iran) have three principal foreign policy aims: to push the US, Satanic foe of the 1979 revolution, out of the Middle East; maintain regional pre-eminence; and strengthen key alliances with China and Russia. Israel's destruction, real or rhetorical, is a fourth* (Simon Tisdall, The Guardian, 2024). Could Russia and China be unwitting midwives in their alliances that birth the AntiChrist or make a way for him?

6th Draft Interpretation

It is God who gives us the secret door keys that unlock the vital vaults of revelation to fully illuminate the dream. It was revealed to me that the dark suit the man was wearing is symbolic of a dark suit—spades and clubs, in a deck of cards. God simply whispered: 'dark card suit.' I had no idea what He was

185

talking about as I do not play cards. I was familiar with the word 'deck,' But apart from that word the decks were clear! After researching online I discovered that the four suits in a deck of cards have a unique symbolism[13]. In particular here, the black (or dark) suits represent the powers of darkness and more specifically can represent a warrior (spade) or agriculture (club). These two meanings spoke to me as the current conflicts (Ukraine and the middle east) are having a significant impact on food production and distribution globally. Further there have been significant protests recently in Europe and elsewhere by farmers who say that their jobs (food production) are being made increasingly more difficult by government restrictions and policy.

I was made aware that the bear swimming around in the world (sea) with the woman symbolic of Europe, was seemingly unable to find its place. Putin has not been able to find his seat at the table with western countries, so he has found his seat with Iran and China and these alliances have formed. The woman swam under the bear given she was dominated by Russia and blocked by the black line (border) between them. Russia's war in Ukraine contributed to a doubling of arms purchases in Europe in 2019–23 relative to 2014–18—there were double sets of 'arms in my dream[14]. Every detail of a dream like this is significant and we must train ourselves to remember everything or pray that God will quicken every essential element to our memories.

---

[13] https://public.websites.umich.edu/~umfandsf/symbolismproject/symbolism.html/C/cards.html

[14] https://www.sipri.org/media/press-release/2024/european-arms-imports-nearly-double-us-and-french-exports-rise-and-russian-exports-fall-sharply

Also in the 6th period of mulling over, studying and seeking God for the dream, God reminded me that the later dream I had on the same night of the dream was of a Chinese child and was a further episode of the dream rather than a separate dream. I, a symbol of a prophet and teacher in the church, was teaching the child to walk—the Chinese church is relatively new and there is a very real need that we pray for the walk of this persecuted yet faithful and powerful church so they can 'stand up' to the spiritual forces of darkness in their country. We should learn from this suffering and sacrificial church too. It's reciprocal: the church in the west is comparatively weak compared to the persecuted church. I was engaged with this child too: learning in return. The child was then by a bed and I was teaching it to read. I believe there is a need for the Chinese church to be taught to 'read' or learn how to decode dreams and visions as there is for the worldwide body of the ecclesia. This is part of the solution to the dream's problem. Praying for the Chinese church to continue to grow in maturity and for it to learn to understand dreams as symbolised by reading (understanding) and the bed (place of dreams).

7th Draft of Interpretation

I felt God warn me that 'the writing is on the wall,' in terms of the phase the world is in. He then took me back to the thick black geometric block and reminded me that I viewed the globe from above. As if I was looking down from outer space, and given its geometric nature, I realised I was seeing a weapon of war and given it was in the sea I looked up submarines. The block if viewed from above, looked exactly like a Russian nuclear submarine. The woman representing Europe was in 'western dress': a smart white shirt and blue skirt; blonde, styled hair. Blue is

187

the colour of heavenly revelation; white is symbolic of the people of God. God, and angels appear in white in the Bible. By stark contrast, satan is symbolised by black in the dream (black cards and the man in the dark suit); but also as in things are stark: the world is increasingly becoming polarised into black and white; good and evil. The yellow colour of the woman's hair is emblematic too. Yellow can denote the presence or glory of God but can also symbolise the end times. Yellow is symbolic of judgement and the tribulation in the Bible, synonymous as it is with brimstone. As is hair: hair is 'covering', in this case the covering over Europe. The angels I have encountered in dreams were blonde. Whether the woman represents the angel over Europe or is simply a symbol of Europe does not change the message or the application of the dream. The dream is a warning of Russian aggression towards Europe as signified by the submarine; the bear that transforms into a man at the gates of the White House is a threat to the USA. As such, Russia is a threat to Europe, and also to America. The 'enemy at the gates' is Russia and her new alliances with the Islamic state of Iran and China: the three empires represented in the dream. Russia is already at the gates of Europe and America. The two pregnant empires indicate what is to come and how to prepare for what satan is birthing through these nations, given there is a 'new world order' emerging. Europe and America are seen as a threat to Russia, China and Iran and they are a threat to us. The countries that control arms, oil, gas and grain will gain control in the world. The food crisis that began with Ukraine and Covid, has sent prices soaring. Iran and Russia have circumvented the west in making their own oil, gas and arms deals. But the immediate threat is that Russia, the immediate 'enemy at the gates,' who has now become the world player it always wanted to become despite the rejection of America, has found its own way onto the world stage by falling 'into the arms' of Iran and China. Russia, now a key player, has its dark suit of cards that it is now dealing: agricultural and military cards that can continue to change the world order drastically unless Europe and America wake up and perceive the enemy at the gate. I initially sensed Antichrist when I saw the bear turn into a man. At this stage, I now understand the man who came from the bear as ushering in a new dark age, the age that gives rise to the antichrist (not the actual figure of the Antichrist but a prefiguring if you will). The pregnant beasts signify other countries that will conform to type and join these alliances, polarising the world still further, and I believe the antichrist will come through one of the countries associated or 'birthed by the leopard: somewhere in the Middle East, Turkey or maybe North Africa. With the Ukraine war, the world has shifted into a dark age and it's rapidly drawing to its conclusion.

Jesus told them this parable: "Look at the fig tree and all the trees. When they sprout leaves, you can see for yourselves and know that summer is near. Even so, when you see these things happening, you know that the kingdom of God is near," (Luke 21, 29–31).

As a final punctuation, if you like, God spoke to me through Shakespeare's soliloquy from Richard III, (spoken by Gloucester). Note that the revelation I received was not Shakespeare's intent when he wrote it! His soliloquy speaks of post war events and familial intrigues. He's not a time traveler though his words can be! Note the relevant symbolism—relevant to the dream; not the original context by Shakespeare. The phrase 'winter of our discontent,' is synonymous with political and social unrest, whatever season of the year; 'winter' is a metaphor for a bleak, discouraging period of time, particularly in the UK where it can be grey, grim, damp and rainy. 'Discontent' implies turmoil and looming threat. I believe we are entering a winter season: the final epoch—the winter of the ages—though there is much more to come. I do believe we are entering 'the winter of time,' where the world is being set up for the Antichrist.

*Now is the **winter of our discontent*** (I am praying about events leading up to winter 2024. The next months are very key. God spoke to me of urgency and grace in May: Mayday and 'may': events 'may' change if people pray! But we need to pray for strength for all of us as we enter our winter season in terms of world timing)
*Made glorious summer by this sun of **York***; (UK)
*And all the clouds that lour'd upon our **house*** (church)
*In the **deep bosom of the ocean buried**.*
*Now are our brows bound with victorious **wreaths**;*
*Our **bruised arms** hung up for monuments;*
*Our stern **alarums*** (alarms/warning) changed (if we pray) to merry meetings,
*Our **dreadful marches** to delightful measures.* (war)
Grim-visaged war hath smooth'd his wrinkled front (face of war)

Application of the dream

- The submarine symbolises a potential attack by sea. Given I heard *'From Russia With Love I Fly to You*, we need to pray about air defences as well including disruptions with satellites, flights and GPS. Russia lies like the snake, though it is now 'hiding in plain sight' like the leopard and the snake. These three new empires that have formed have given Iran the boldness to attack Israel and Russia the audacity to attack Ukraine and China to flex its muscles in Taiwan. They are 'arming' themselves for the future and ready to birth according to type: other people and countries will

190

be drawn in of similar skin or fur, ie. 'satanic covering' to the leopard and snake. We need to be 'armed' with the right hand of God to pray, intercede and intercept as God directs.

- Europe and America need to act decisively and this is how we need to pray. America desperately needs wise government, as does Europe. Empires are rising to take its place.

- America (and the Christian world) need a strong church to fend off the enemy at the gates, but the two administrations are involved in their own petty intrigues while the enemy flexes its muscles *at the gates.* Now! Post Covid Britain was involved in its own domino effect political farce. We cannot be partisan but must pray as a believing 'clan.' We cannot be sitting ducks bobbing about on the waters of the world while dark forces take control.

- We need to pray for Europe's covering as signified by the blonde hair of the woman. Angelic protection and the prayers of the saints. See my daughter's dream on what happened after The Queen died.

- Pray for the church in the west to become as resolute as the persecuted church in China. We know suffering is coming. We must be strong and be prepared to 'get uncomfortable' enough to be one strong unified miracle working entity.

- The satanic, counterfeit religion is also 'at the gates,' I believe, even now, the Antichrist is incubating, in the pregnant beasts. Fundamentalist Islam seeks to unify the world via a worldwide caliphate. We know the Antichrist will arise with his message of peace and there will be a false prophet. The recent war in Israel has brought much suffering to, and sympathy for, the Palestinian people and thereby witting and unwitting support for islam, even to the point of excusing and supporting what islamic extremists did to Israel on 7th October 2023. We need to pray for more dreams and visions for Muslim people as have been recently reported.

- We must pray for Israel, whatever our opinion of their leadership is. Controversial leadership is nothing new; it is in Jerusalem that the final battles will take place. Jesus is Jewish and so are we by adoption. Israel needs prayers for peace and protection and for wise leadership.

Bear the words of Jesus our saviour in mind regarding the signs of the times: Luke 21:10–36. There is much more to come and much more praying to be done.

Keep documenting and mining your dreams even if they do not make full sense. Even if you don't get everything right it will be documented for you to realign or make sense of when you are more skilled in the future, or when God has revealed what He wants to reveal in the fulness of time. They may even speak of historical events to come. Dreams like this wake us up to what's happening in the world so that we can gain strategy to pray as God directs. Thank God, that His is the final word on all matters.

Chapter 17. Interpretation Toolkit

After the 'heaviness' of the last chapter I would like to remind us that God sits on His throne and laughs while the nations plot in vain! He is in control and given we are seated in heavenly places with Him and dreaming heavenly dreams, there is much that we can do to change the course of history, if only we will wake up to His strategies! We must maintain the joy that is our strength and being creative as He is helps enormously. God is creative and so are we. God is also logical, and mathematical, which is why your symbols will add up to make logical sense, but, as we see from what is on earth and the cosmos, He is infinitely creative. The more creative you are the more adept you will become at dream interpretation—see Daniel's skillset and abilities. Be a scholar of the Bible to develop your brain. Being 'transformed by the renewing of your mind' will actually create brain plasticity and new neural pathways. Basically reading and learning the word of God so that it becomes innate—the word made flesh in you—will make you a boffin or more boffiny than you already are. All aboard the Boffinada! Similarly, decoding dreams, and learning to decode them—learning the creative *lingua franca* of God, will make you more creative and creativity is such a valuable tool for life and health that I will be writing another book on that subject alone. There are strong links between dreamers and creativity. "Sleep is not just vital to health but perhaps the greatest single source of creativity," explains Alex Tew, co-founder of Calm. According to a paper published on the National Library of Medicine "the creation of novel associations between different waking-life experiences during dreaming may also bolster creativity." [15] How brilliant is our God, the designer of sleep, dreams and creativity?

In her introduction to her 1818 novel *Frankenstein's Monster* Mary Wollstonecraft Shelley wrote this: "When I placed my head upon my pillow, I did not sleep, nor could I be said to think... I saw—with shut eyes, but acute mental vision—I saw the pale student of unhallowed arts kneeling beside the thing he had put together. I saw the hideous phantasm of a man stretched out, and then, on the working of some powerful engine, show signs of life, and stir with an uneasy, half-vital motion. Frightful must it be; for supremely frightful would be the effect of any human endeavour to mock the stupendous Creator of the world." One might argue this novel was demonically inspired, but those of us who have studied the 19th Century novel have all read it, it is one of the seminal works and required syllabus reading of Gothic English Literature. *Yesterday* by Paul McCartney, was written at the Wimpole Street home of his then girlfriend Jane Asher and her family during the filming of *Help!* Waking from a dream, he initially thought the melody was him remembering an old song. He went to the piano to play it, so that he would be able to recall it (which is why you need to record your dreams). As he later said: "For about a month I went round to people in the music business and asked them whether they had ever heard it before. Eventually it became like handing something in to the police. I thought if no one claimed it after a few weeks then I could have it." It became the song many of us know and love. It certainly seems as though it's here to stay (sorry). The surrealist master Salvador Dali described his paintings as "hand-painted dream photographs."

---

[15] https://www.ncbi.nlm.nih.gov/pmc/articles/PMC10091095/

Dreams utilise visionary thinking or abstract thinking. We use intuition as well as logic to interpret dreams or abstract and concrete thinking. If you consider yourself creative you will find creative ways of interpreting a joy. If you consider yourself not to be creative, which is not true, you are just out of practise, (show me an unschooled child that won't draw) you might find some of the exercises peculiar at first but I encourage you to have a go as it will help build your creative or intuitive thinking processes so you can better function as a creative child of a creative God which will impact the whole of your life as well as make you a more skilful dream interpreter. Interpreting dreams can be a serious business but need not be onerous. It can be fun and should be illustrated as such when teaching children. I've designed some fun dream interpretation methods to help you think more creatively, all the better to help you understand the language of dreams better. The methods I am going to suggest will have KF next to them for the ones that are kid friendly or KFA meaning kid friendly if adapted. Most of my dreams have drawings, cartoons, or doodling all over them. Often they are sectioned in circles and boxes that link together. When I see an image I have drawn, it usually triggers the memory of the whole dream. Visual language is like this. Being creative is also highly therapeutic and meditative, so you will be doing yourself a holistic favour if you follow the exercises. It is helpful to see your dream laid out before you as you will see if you choose to try some of the upcoming strategies that map the dream out before you in words or pictures—doodling or drawing—rather than in dense text that can 'bog you down.' It can be helpful to try various methodologies as you learn, but you will discover what works for you. They are fun too and laughter is good for your health!

Mind Maps

Mind mapping is a way of spilling the contents of your head on a page. You can use words and statements in circles or speech bubbles or shapes. You can draw or use text and colour. Get creative. The more creatively you represent the elements of your dream the more creative you will become! Sometimes I draw people and doodle symbols and this helps me further remember the dream later. You don't need to be an artist to do this, you can use stick men or simple drawings. As I doodle and note down phrases and bits of interpretation with question marks, the dream's meaning begins to emerge and it gives space for the Holy Spirit to speak. Get out of the prescriptive box. It's good to be a lateral thinker. You can draw a heart in the middle to symbolise the central focus of your dream and branch out with lines and boxes or circles and clouds from there. If you are at the heart of the dream or involved in the action or events of the dream draw shapes for action in different sub-branches; add in any other elements or people. Do one per dream scene if there are lots of scenes. Make notes or little doodles/drawings inside the boxes. Capitalise important words or text. I often doodle with a black pen. It helps things 'bubble up' from the subconscious.

Arrow Method

I use an arrow method a lot if the river of meaning in my brain is flowing quickly: Jane ->. running down the stairs -> afraid -> room dark -> man -> strongman? Chasing her -> red car pulling up -> Jane in car -> mistake! -> countryside. This method utilises 'free association.' It is flow, still creative, but not in the sense of 'now I'm drawing.' Your mind is coasting in neutral, freer, more intuitive, which switches off 'judging' or getting overworked. Free association allows symbols to emerge naturally. You can write more carefully afterwards.

Tip: Use a pencil and have a rubber (eraser) handy so you can rub things out if need be.

Doodling or Drawing the Dream

In therapy, Freud encouraged his patients to relax their critical faculties so that free association in a quest for meaning, could arise from the subconscious however incoherently at first. This was how they discussed their dreams with him. Dreams come from the intuitive creative realm, and these are the areas of ourselves that we need to 'switch on' if we are not already tuned into our creative intuitive selves. Drawing your dream or parts of your dream helps you activate the creative parts of your brain. Allowing free association, including 'out of the box' theories or ideas, helps your brain access pathways it wouldn't normally use. It flicks a switch you may not be used to using, that accesses your imagination in new or surprising ways.

Don't judge your drawing. It's between you and God. Enjoy it. It also gives the other parts of your brain, the logical side a rest so that it will reveal more in due course. I draw, write and doodle in my one dream journal, but go right ahead and get a blank paper book for drawing if you fancy. Crack open those coloured fine tip or gel pens too! Or use a pencil and shade and pattern to your heart's content. Drawing helps bring things to mind, especially details or forgotten elements. The sky is not your limit! You can draw where things are—up/down/right/left— situation and placement have meaning too. Right can mean 'right now' and left 'the future.' When I am prophesying over someone I often feel God confirming whether something is for now or the future when I feel Him on my left or right side.

The Puzzle Method

Think of your dream as a puzzle. Write or draw the symbols of your dream over the page so you can clearly see them all and then decode each symbol one by one. Cross them out when decoded. Next, start connecting your decoded symbols with lines in logical sequence: decide which image goes with another. When they do link the 'pieces' together like pieces in a puzzle. As you choose your puzzle pieces: car, woman, tree, road, butcher... see if a bigger picture emerges or if the pieces begin to add up to form a picture. Trust yourself. You can always move things around until a clear picture emerges. Ask the Holy Spirit to tell you the true meaning of a symbol you are stuck on.

Cleaning up Your House

Given most of your dreams are about you, many will take place in a house, known or unknown to you. This exercise is a way of helping you relate surprising elements to yourself. Find the subject or focus of your dream. Draw lines to each object or sub focus of the dream and consider all the symbols or people to be aspects of yourself. For instance, if you see a pot boiling, could that be your temper threatening to bubble up? If there is a calm pool in your dream, consider what it might take for you to reach a state of peace. If there is a blocked pipe or a high wall, what unhelpful emotion or memory is hindering you? If there is a child giggling, consider getting back in touch with your younger joyful self.

Picture Keys

Take out your journal and write down your dream. Draw two columns. Take all the symbols in your dream and draw them in a column—make simple drawings, as long as you recognise them! I draw more clearly than I write—a better verb might be 'scrawl.' Next think of an interpretation that the symbols you have drawn might represent. Draw those in another column next to the dream symbols. While you are drawing, if thoughts and ideas pop into your head draw them as well. If they are tricky to draw write them out with question marks next to your columns.

Bubble Up KF

Draw a series of say four bubbles from the bottom of your paper to the top. Make large bubbles at the bottom getting smaller and smaller as they reach the top of the page, but not so small that you can't write a word in them. Write your first idea for a symbol at the bottom of the page and then steadily let your imagination bubble up with other possible meanings that you place in the smaller and smaller bubbles. Choose the symbol that makes sense in the setting of your dream. God will float ideas up as you do this. Allow all the thoughts to bubble up and then pop the bubbles that don't make sense in the setting of the dream or context of your life: cross them out or rub them out.

Go Fish KF

This is a fun method to use with your children and utilises the free association method. Write the dream out. Divide your page in half. Place all the symbols of your dream in the bottom half of the page in the 'sand' of possibility. On the top half of your page draw a boat shape. 'Catch the fish,' by 'drawing up' ideas for the symbols, put them in simple fish shapes. When you have fished for a catch of symbol ideas choose the ones that best fit into the boat or setting of your dream. Write them onto your boat. Then write your interpretation out with the correct 'fish' or symbols. Then take them home to land in the context of the dreamer's life.

Dream Cards KF

Make yourself a set of dream cards with common dream symbols on them with potential meanings. Draw an apple on the one side for example. On the other side write possible interpretations: knowledge; health etc. Make a collection of cards as you learn to decode meanings. Keep the cards handy to help trigger possible meanings for your dream when you are stuck.

Flowers in the Garden KF

Draw a line across the middle of the page.
Take your list of underlined symbols from your dream that you have written out in your journal. Draw an appropriate amount of flowers. Write each symbol onto a flower. Place the flowers in the garden which is the setting of your life—their flower heads will rise above the line, the stems will dangle under the line and into 'the soil.' Underneath the line, in the soil is your heart, apply the meaning of the symbols here. When you have decoded them all, take them as a bunch and offer the message into the context of your life.

Flower Power

Write out your dream. Underline the symbols. Take a pencil. Draw a large flower on your page with a circle at the centre into which you note the focus or subject of your dream. Then draw about ten petals onto which you will draw your decoded symbols. See which symbols make sense with the others that you see displayed before you. Pick off these petals and write them into the decoded version of your dream that you commit to your journal.

The Circles and Numbers KF

It helps to see your dream spread out over a page in diagram form when you want to decode it as you see things clearly and concisely than if it is in a block of text. Circle and number every step of the unfolding action of your dream across your page, one circle per piece of action or episode at a time. You can then make connections between the episodes of action by linking them with lines. Make notes as you need.

Fuzzy Felt Pelt KF

You will need scissors and a pencil and rubber for this. I'm calling this 'Fuzzy Felt Pelt' as it is inspired by the aforementioned Fuzzy Felt idea. Write out your dream. Draw mountains in the distance and a path leading up to the mountain. Draw an arrow at the base of the path (the bottom of the page) and a cross at the top of the mountain. Draw all the people, animals and objects in your dream on a separate piece of paper and cut them out (you can just draw them in pencil and rub them out if you don't want to cut them out). Take the focus or subject of your dream—most likely you or someone representing you and place them at the start of the road. They are going to be journeying up the road with their companion objects—the other symbols in the dream until they reach the top of the mountain where the dream is fulfilled and all the symbols come together. Place each element of the dream: people, objects etc, along the road and have your dream subject (who or what the dream is about) relate to them. Move the elements around on the road, until they make sense in the dream setting. Write the final meaning on the mountain and the title of the dream at the top of the mountain.

Dream Mapping

Draw your dream symbols or write them down equally spaced out over a page which is your dream map. Say there is a person on a bicycle and a hospital. A person may be on a bicycle cycling to a hospital because they need healing. Therefore the hospital is a symbol of healing for the person. Write down healing next to hospital, and draw a line from the person to the hospital, but if they stop along the way to chat to someone this could signify distraction, note down 'distraction' and draw another line to show you have understood this connection. Keep writing down or or drawing your symbols drawing lines until you have completed your connections.

The Tree KF

This is a good method to use when you need to mine for more revelation. Draw a tree with an appropriate number of extending branches. Write the title of your dream above your tree. Write the focus or subject of the dream on the trunk. Then write the unfolding action onto branches. Other elements can be written onto subsidiary branches. As more revelation comes following prayer and biblical/any other research put it into leaves on the appropriate branch of your tree.

Dream Clouds

Free association method. After writing out the dream in your journal, write your dream symbols in an appropriate number of clouds. Draw a number of subsidiary clouds linked to the main cloud with possible meanings. Once you have figured out which clouds are appropriate in the sky of your setting, ground the meaning into the context of your life.

Cluedo Method KFA

In order to use this light-hearted method you are going to indulge in a little role-play and turn yourself into a detective. Say you have a dream in which someone is murdered. Usually when someone is murdered in a dream, it is a part of themselves that needs to die in order for heart progress to be made. If you imagine your dream as a crime scene, put the 'murdered' person in the centre of a sheet of paper. Draw a box around them to indicate them being taped off by crime scene tape. Then place the objects of the dream, which may be other people or elements around them. Place other events of the dream around the square in boxes. Perhaps it's you who needs to die to aspects of self, for your God designed personhood to really shine through. Now begin to pose questions. What aspect of you needs to die to self? (John 3: 3–7) You might see yourself taking an undue amount of time staring in a mirror putting on make up; buying too many shoes or clothes, or arguing? What is the function of something? Shoes can indicate shod feet ready to bring the good news, but dusty feet could mean: shake off the dust and leave that situation! What do you need to let go of in life as symbolised by the scenes or objects—such as the mirror or the make up—in the dream? Are you caring too much about how you look to others? (Not that there's anything wrong with make up!). You might see bottles of wine littered across a road, blocking your progress. A sign to give up drinking!

Out of the Box KF

This is a way to quickly use the shutter of your mind to click on potentially relevant information from your subconscious. Unless you've been looking the other way you will have heard the expression 'out of the box' thinking. Creative people tend to be 'out of the box,' and some of us question everything and put it all to the test: school systems, political systems, the lot. I'm not suggesting you have a brain transplant here, but I do suggest you try to 'get out of your head,' as it were in a healthy way. As in, I want to disrupt your usual way of thinking to make you think more creatively. Take your dream and write it in your dream journal. Take your symbols and write them down. Underline them. Draw boxes for each symbol. Name the boxes. Then, without thinking brainstorm as many ideas as you can think of and write them in the box. Do not think much about what you are drawing up from the depths of your imagination. Free associate, let your mind loose like a balloon and see what floats up. You are not going to apply your thinking skills straight away, but if something rings true or resonates as a symbol write it down. See if any resonate with your dream. If they don't, don't despair. You are exercising your creative brain which is going to help you become more creative and thus a better dream interpreter! Once you have done the same for all the symbols, make them permanent by fixing them in your interpretation (and your journal) and apply it to your life as a final test.

Dream Kites, Dream Butterflies, Dream Balloons and Dream Balls... the possibilities are endless KF

You can draw butterflies and kites out on a sheet of paper and photocopy them. When your child has a dream, they can simply write their dream symbols into kites and butterflies or balloons or footballs which will find their way into a football net once decoded. Why not come up with your own creative methodology for dreams? Keep an eye on my website for more dream interpretation ideas and for further books and upcoming workbooks for kids and adults.

Final Questions & Other Considerations

I have so many dreams I don't know what to do with them!

"For when dreams increase and words grow many, there is vanity; but God is the one you must fear." Ecclesiastes 5:7 ESV

When one has lots of dreams, it is often the mind processing. This can be due to conflict between the soul and spirit or when there is anxiety or stress present. Write them all down and take them to God. After prayer try to see if any of the images or scenes make sense. What is the setting of the dream—does that make sense? Then apply them to the context of your life. You may just find the answer you have been looking for. "As when a hungry man dreams, and behold, he is eating, and awakes with his hunger not satisfied, or as when a thirsty man dreams, and behold, he is drinking, and awakes faint, with his thirst not quenched, so shall the multitude of all the nations be that fight against Mount Zion." (Isaiah 29:8 ESV). You can simply dream of water when you are thirsty or breakfast when you are hungry! There is no need to make a meal out of these dreams! But sometimes God is saying more. Don't discount anything. Drink more water, as by the time you are thirsty your body is already dehydrated. God wants you fit and well in body mind and spirit, given you are a temple of the Holy Spirit. Don't neglect any part of yourself. God has made the complex machine of your body with a 100 year warranty but if you put the wrong fuel in the tank or not enough of it in, you could find yourself breaking down on the side of the road, unable to continue your journey! He cares about our bodies, minds and spirits and we should too.

I never remember my dreams!

"In a dream, in a vision of the night, when deep sleep falls on people as they slumber in their beds." (Job 33:15)

We all dream. This has been scientifically proven. Sometimes God delivers a dream to our spirit but we do not yet have the spiritual capacity or character to fulfil the message of the dream. The dream is deposited in you and will stay in seed form until you have grown enough to make a withdrawal on the deposit that God has placed in you. You grow into your capacity to dream and remember them, as you diligently seek the dream giver and become a diligent student of dreams and visions. Pray before sleeping and ask God to help you remember your dreams. Have paper and pen ready and follow procedure! God is faithful.

I don't dream

You do. You just don't remember them. Neurobiology has demonstrated that, although all of us dream every night, not everybody remembers what he or she has dreamt[16]. I lay hands on people who say they don't dream and they begin to. Place your hands on your head, repent of your unbelief and ask God to help you recall your dream tonight. Be expectant. Everything in the Kingdom of God is received through faith and sometimes faith is tested through patience. Don't give

---

[16] https://www.ncbi.nlm.nih.gov/pmc/articles/PMC9171870/

up. Again, show you are prepared with dream journal or notebook and pen and recording device at the ready by your bed.

The Family Anointing & Children

Never think your children are too young to hear from God. Children are very discerning in the spirit. My eldest child, whose name means 'light' has always been able to discern what is going on with people. As a child he gave me such vivid prophecies they are tattooed on my mind. My second son, the one who saw the two lions, sees vividly in the spirit and in dreams and is affected by the spiritual atmosphere in houses. My daughter has open visions, at three she saw a lion at a well known 'thin place' in Wales. She was terrified! My youngest son has an inner 'knowing' when something is up. He can tell if someone is sad no matter how hard they try to cover their emotions up. When he was very little he would run from a room in terror if a statue of buddha was in it or in the garden as there sometimes was in the houses or gardens of unbelievers we visited. All of my children and my husband dream. They have been 'schooled' in dream interpretation as I have always written of and spoken about dreams, so they do too. We discuss and interpret dreams most mornings over breakfast. There is a family anointing to dream. All of them are interpreters of their own dreams, usually with my help. Increasingly, we all help each other. The anointing for dreams seems to increase when anointed interpreters are present, as is the case when a company of prophets gets together and the anointing to prophesy increases. Don't be surprised if as you are faithful to record your dreams, and discuss them with your family so that they will begin to dream too! Get ready to pass it all on, interpret together, and soon we will have that Joel prophecy nailed!

Impartation

I speak at events on dreams where I usually pray and impart the ability to dream. I am happy to report that I have yet to encounter a dreamer who has failed to dream after I have prayed a prayer of impartation.

If you would like me to speak at your church or event, wherever it is in the world, I will be happy to do so. Please contact me at: ej@ejhillman.com

Let's all wake up to the fact that God is speaking all the time and that all we need to do is 'tune in' to hear His voice. Dreams and visions and the wisdom they carry should be a part of everyday lives on earth not just something we read about, and not something we should be missing out on, or something for the future. We can access heaven on earth today and live out of the wisdom God imparts through dreams today. This is your invitation to engage with this powerful eternal kingdom dynamic. As Eleanor Roosevelt said: "The future belongs to those who believe in the beauty of their dreams." Happy Dreaming!

Symbology Key for the meaning of the parable:

Adopted — We are adopted by the eternal king
War — the war for God's family
Home — home is in the eternal kingdom of heaven
Middle-East — Land of Zion; where Israel is situated —symbolic of our eternal home
Family ripped apart — The enemy seeks to divide God's family
Father — God
Fight in the war — The war for the spirits of the people of God
Emigrated — Leave our eternal home to be on earth
Office — Place of learning
Park — Place of rest and reflection
Lunch break —Spiritual food taken at rest at the centre of your day or life
Beautiful birds — Symbolic here of dreams; birds fly in the high places; pigeons carry messages and soar in the high places
Magnificence & diversity — God's creations are magnificent and infinitely diverse
Old Man — Holy Spirit; your 'old man' dreams dreams
Traveller passing through — A man from an eternal Kingdom
Birds loved him — His creation loves Him; the dreams He gives reflect Him
Feed from his hands — Take His spiritual food
Fed from Joanna's hands — Feed on what He gives you through the revelation you receive through dreams and pass it on!
Countries he'd been to — The realms; heavens and the earth

His words remained in her: His words are spirit and life. "They landed in her heart."

Particular situations in her life — in dreams God directs us specifically and personally

Mysterious yet familiar — God is both mysterious and familiar to us: we are made in the image of God *imago dei*

Going to park less and less — Cares of this world

Long time — The danger of spiritual erosion

Inheritance — Our inheritance in God

Lawyer — We are purchased legally by His blood

Wax seal — Heavenly seal

Crown — King

Home country — Heaven

Birthday — New birth

Banquet — Symbolic of the great banquet to come; but an earthly 'feast' is nothing to the one to come

Invitation to a party — God hopes to be invited to 'sup' or commune with us

Hope — Eternal hope; God hopes as we do

Invitation — To 'dine' with us

Suit — Groom for the bride of Christ that Joanna is symbolic of

Remember Him — God wants us to remember Him in all things

Candle light — Jesus is the light of the world

Feast — Symbolic of the great fest to come

Growing emptiness — The emptiness one feels without God

Plenty but lack — Riches and plenty cannot compensate for the riches of the spirit

Windows — Windows of the soul

Realised what was missing — Epiphany or revelation

Outside — Separated from God

As she opened the door, the man was coming up the path — He pursues us with His love

she held out her hand to him and he reached out for hers — Drawn near to God and He will draw near to you.

Ring on His finger with crown — Jesus, the groom from the eternal kingdom

This is not an exhaustive list. There is yet more symbolic language. See if you can decode the rest.

May you be richly blessed in your pursuit of learning to go deeper in dream interpretation.

www.ingramcontent.com/pod-product-compliance
Lightning Source LLC
La Vergne TN
LVHW052023080426
835513LV00018B/2126